The Eight Temples Meditation Project

Rawn Clark

2002

The Eight Temples Meditation Project.
by Rawn Clark.

Achevé d'imprimer sur rotative par l'imprimerie Darantiere à Dijon-Quetigny en juillet 2002
Dépôt légal : juillet 2002 - N° d'impression 22-0938

CONTENTS

INTRODUCTION

That ancient challenge, "know thyself", is the primary call to arms for those seeking self-realization or initiation into the Mysteries. The great error many make is in assuming that self-knowledge is just an internal thing. But quite the contrary is true, for the 'self' we are trying to discover is ultimately an infinite, all-encompassing, universal being. To truly "know thyself" is to know that all is Self.

It is for this reason that a path of initiation seeks to correlate the inner, personal world of the psyche, with the outer, physical world. These all-too-often disparate realms are woven together by taking full advantage of their commonalities in structure. With the tools of analogy and symbolism in hand, the initiate artfully traces the lines of causality that naturally exist between what is experienced internally and what is experienced externally.

The initiate achieves this by pursuing self-examination concurrent with a disciplined study of the external universe. Each is pursued with the other in mind. In other words, universal principles are studied and applied to the work of self-examination. Likewise, personal principles, learned from self-examination, are applied to the work of understanding the external world. Joined in this way, the outer illumines the inner and vise versa.

A classic example is the work with the Four Elements outlined by Franz Bardon in his excellent book, Initiation Into Hermetics. Here, the Elements are explored and employed in two ways. One is external and involves certain meditational practices which lead to an experiential understanding of the Elements as universal forces. The second, concurrent way is internal, wherein the universal-Elements are used as an analytic structure, a template which guides the examination of the inner personality-self. This second usage correlates the universal-Elements with the personal-Elements at a very practical, experiential level.

Throughout history, the essential process of self-realization has been draped over a vast number of different philosophical structures, each one symbolizing a specific understanding of the universe. It is more the presence of structure, than the nature of the specific structure chosen, that determines success. Thus a Catholic is just as likely to achieve Self-realization as is a Buddhist or a Wiccan or a Qabbalist or an Aboriginal Shaman, to name just a small few of the many options manifest throughout the world.

This is not to say that the type of structure is unimportant. For without a doubt, the philosophical specifics of any given structure will influence the details of the process of self-realization. The point is that a structure can either limit your experience or open it to expansion; depending however, not so much upon the structure itself, as upon how you approach that structure and what you do with it.

The eight meditations which follow serve as very practical introductions to the specific structure of Western Hermetic Qabbalah. Each of the meditations is an experience that illumines both the inner and outer significance of the realms explored. Here, the essentially internal process of meditation is focused upon factors which directly concern the meditator's external life circumstance.

The eight astra-mental Temples outlined in the series are designed to become lifelong tools. Each one has practical applications for both the initiate's internal and external work. Once introduced to the Temples, the initiate is free to return to them at any time and pursue further, more detailed work. Thus the astra-mental Temples themselves, as well as the initiate's relationship with them, evolve over time. With repeated usage, their inherent structure aligns the initiate's inner and outer worlds, and establishes the solid, integral foundation which serves as the initiate's springboard to continual self-expansion.

Project Outline

The 8 Temples Meditation Project evolved out of an earlier project in which a small group of us experimented with meeting regularly at an astra-mental locale. That original experiment ran for two years (Nov.'95 through Dec.'97), during which time we learned many valuable, and ultimately practical, lessons about the astra-mental realm itself and about meeting there. [For more information along these lines, see "Beneath an Astral Moon", located in the appendix.]

As the experimental phase of our work together came to a conclusion, I considered instigating a new project, one based not upon learning new lessons, but upon proving out and making good use of the lessons we had already learned.

Around that same point in time, two different friends spoke of their desire to learn more about the Qabbalistic Tree of Life and about the practical meanings of the planetary symbols. So, I designed the Project to incorporate both the aforementioned lessons about astra-mental time-space, and my own knowledge of practical Qabbalah and astrology.

6

The 8 Temples Meditation Project ran for eight months -- starting with the late-December, 1997 new moon and ending with the early-August, 1998 full moon. Around the day of the new moon each of the participants received a packet of information in the mail. These "New Moon Packets" each contained an explanatory introduction and an outline of the upcoming meditation.

The meditations were scheduled on or near each month's full moon, so all the participants had two weeks to study the written material. During those two weeks, I constructed the astra-mental Temples and then I conducted the meditation ritual as scheduled.

Within a week after the meditation, each of the participants submitted a report detailing their experiences. Copies of these reports were then forwarded to the participants in the following New Moon Packet. This particular practice allowed for two things: 1) It allowed each participant to see what others had experienced. 2) It allowed me to gauge the effectiveness of what I was doing, as I was doing it. Each month I analyzed the reports in receipt and used that information to fine-tune the upcoming meditation.

The Project followed a standard "Path of Return" approach to the Qabbalistic Tree of Life. The meditations began with sphere 10, Malkuth/Earth, and worked up the Tree to sphere 3, Binah/Saturn. Each meditation built upon the experiences of the one preceding it, so there is a clear continuity throughout the series.

One desire I held for the Project was that it would achieve a balance between "script" and "spontaneity". On the one hand, the earlier group work had taught me how powerful a focusing influence a pre-determined structure can have upon an astra-mental meeting. But on the other hand was the equally clear lesson that only spontaneity can raise such a structure from the level of "theatrical delusion" to the realm of true magic. Therefore, each of the meditations includes a period of un-scripted, self-directed time, during which the participant interacts spontaneously with the environment at hand.

I am a magician. For me, this Project is a work of magic. After finalizing their design, each of these eight Temples were ritually constructed out of the astra-mental substance, using all the various magics I am familiar with. Their individual construction took anywhere from an hour to several months to complete, varying radically from Temple to Temple.

Not only the Temples themselves had to be constructed, but also the connections between the Temples had to be established. Furthermore, the Temples had to be truly joined with the realms that they symbolize.

7

I used a specific structure in establishing the connections between the Temples. For this, I designed a specific sequence of visualizations, actions and spoken words, that unlocks the connections between specific realms. By following this induction sequence, one accesses the chosen Temple. The first time that one pursues the induction, one is led directly to an experience of the introductory meditation ritual.

This brings me to the issue of time. Astra-mental space-time is not quite like physical space-time. It is a much more fluid, malleable thing.

Physical time is a measurable constant -- we can clock its passage. Astra-mental time however, is not constant in the same way physical time is. For example, the passage of one hour's physical time can be experienced anywhere between the poles of in-the-blink-of-an-eye and ages-and-ages. This is the astra-mental component of time -- an immeasurable, experiential thing defined not by a clock's ticking, but by the quality and quantity of one's personal attention and intention.

It is possible to so enhance the astra-mental aspects of a specific moment of physical time (working through the now-ness of the present-moment) as to result in its preservation. What is preserved is that moment's quality of real-time, present-moment now-ness -- a quality that is generally lost as we move further away in time from the incidents contained within any given past-moment of time-space. When applied to a span of time (a connected series of present-moments) this process of enhancement and preservation is called "encapsulation".

Yes, I know, that's a complex string of concepts I have just strung for you! To simplify: I have so designed these meditations that the real-time enactment of these rituals has been preserved astra-mentally. Since I encapsulated the astra-mental component of each of the Project's hour-long meditation rituals, by simply following the induction sequence of visualizations, etc., you will be led directly to the encapsulated hour itself and actually participate in the outlined ritual as it was originally performed.

This was born out in two different ways during the Project. The first was that we perceived a nearly countless swarm of individuals attending our meditation rituals from future points in time-space. These were clearly folks, like yourself, who were reading these words and pursuing these meditations from within a present-moment that had yet to occur when the meditation rituals themselves were performed. Nonetheless, your presences were all accounted for and engaged during the real-time enactment of those rituals. In several instances these "future-folk" played important roles in the shared,

8

group experience!

The second evidence that the encapsulation of each meditation was successful, is the experience of those participants who, for one reason or another, were unable to participate on the scheduled night and ended up pursuing the meditation a few days or a week later. Without fail, they were able to access a real-time experience of the original meditation ritual.

The eight Temple meditations which follow are meant only as introductions to these astra-mental realms. They merely acquaint one with the terrain and with the tools available for working there. In light of this fact, each of the meditation outlines is followed by suggestions for future, solitary work.

The structure of these meditations is such that once introduced, you are free to re-visit the Temples at any time you choose. An analysis of the Project reports reveals that for each of the original participants, the eight Temples have become handy tools to which they return frequently in pursuit of their ongoing, spontaneous inner work. I pray that you too will find them of lasting value.

Overview of Symbols

The Qabbalistic Tree of Life originated over 2,000 years ago (some say over 6,000 years ago) in the context of the Jewish mystical tradition, and has been a core part of the Western Hermetic tradition for at least 500 years. Today, there are many variations of Qabbalistic symbolism in use, ranging from the strictly Jewish Kabbalah, to the strictly Christian Cabala.

The variation employed for this series of eight meditations will be a fairly simple Western Hermetic approach -- heavy on the Hebrew and Pagan, and light on the Christian, as is my way. However, the emphasis here will be less upon magic per se, and more upon spiritual growth.

The first step is to familiarize yourself with the following diagram and table of correspondences. You needn't memorize them, just acquaint yourself with them.

9

Qabbalistic Tree of Life

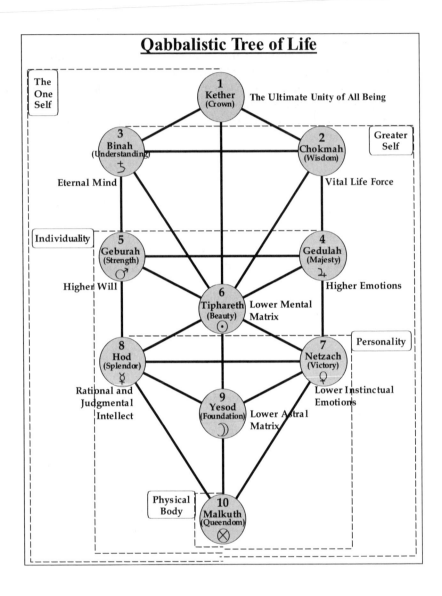

The One Self

The Ultimate Unity of All Being

Greater Self

Eternal Mind

Vital Life Force

Individuality

Higher Will

Higher Emotions

Lower Mental Matrix

Personality

Rational and Judgmental Intellect

Lower Instinctual Emotions

Lower Astral Matrix

Physical Body

1 Kether (Crown)

3 Binah (Understanding)

2 Chokmah (Wisdom)

5 Geburah (Strength)

4 Gedulah (Majesty)

6 Tiphareth (Beauty)

8 Hod (Splendor)

7 Netzach (Victory)

9 Yesod (Foundation)

10 Malkuth (Queendom)

Table of Correspondences

Qabbalistic Sphere:	Astro Sphere:	God/dess Name (Password):	8 Planetary Temples:	Color & Stone:
#1 Kether (Crown)	Universe	Eheieh אהיה "I am"	----	White Brilliance & Diamond.
#2 Chokmah (Wisdom)	Zodiac	Yah יה "The One"	----	Pale Gray & Star Ruby.
#3 Binah (Understanding)	Saturn	IHVH Elohim יהוה אלהים "Supreme God"	Three-sided Temple of Limitation.	Black & Obsidian.
#4 Gedulah (Majesty)	Jupiter	El אל "God"	Four-sided Temple of Mercy.	Bright Blue & Lapis Lazuli.
#5 Geburah (Strength)	Mars	Elohim Gibor אלהים גבור "God of Might"	Five-sided Temple of Severity.	Scarlet Red & Ruby.
#6 Tiphareth (Beauty)	Sun	IHVH Adonai יהוה אדני "Supreme Lord"	Twelve-sided Temple of the Sun.	Yellow Gold & Topaz.
#7 Netzach (Victory)	Venus	IHVH Tzabauth יהוה צבאות "Supreme Legions"	Seven-sided Temple of Emotions.	Bright Green & Emerald.
#8 Hod (Splendor)	Mercury	Elohim Tzabauth אלהים צבאות "God of Legions"	Eight-sided Temple of Learning.	Bright Orange & Fire Opal.
#9 Yesod (Foundation)	Moon	Shaddai שדי "Almighty"	Nine-sided Temple of the Personality.	Violet or Silver & Amethyst.
#10 Malkuth (Queendom)	Earth	Adonai אדני "Lord"	Four-sided Temple of the Elements.	Mixtures & Smokey Quartz.

The Hebrew Alphabet

Letter	Name	Value	Definition	Equivalent
א	Aleph	1	Ox or Bull	A
ב	Beth	2	House	B or V
ג	Gimel	3	Camel	G or Gh
ד	Daleth	4	Door	D or Dh
ה	He	5	Window	H
ו	Vav	6	Nail	V, O or U
ז	Zayin	7	Sword	Z
ח	Cheth	8	Fenced Field	Ch (glottal)
ט	Teth	9	Coiled Serpent	T
י	Yod	10	Finger or Hand	Y
כ ך	Kaph	20/500	Cupped Hand or Palm	K or Kh
ל	Lamed	30	Oxgoad or Prod	L
מ ם	Mem	40/600	Water	M
נ ן	Nun	50/700	Fish	N
ס	Samekh	60	Tent Stake or Prop	S
ע	Ayin	70	Eye or Spring	O
פ ף	Peh	80/800	Mouth	P or Ph
צ ץ	Tzaddi	90/900	Fish Hook	Tz or C
ק	Qooph	100	Back of Head	Q
ר	Resh	200	Head or Face	R
ש	Shin	300	Teeth	Sh or S
ת	Tav	400	Cross	T or Th

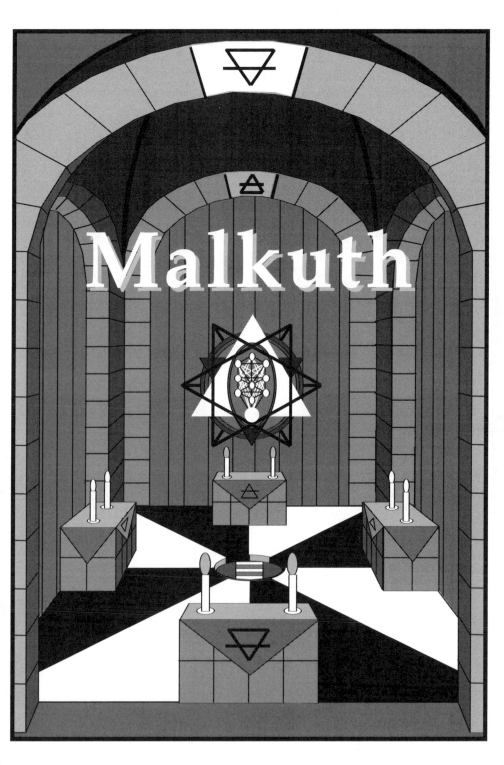

Introduction

The Hebrew word Malkuth (pronounced "mal-cooth"), is generally translated into English as "kingdom", though in my opinion, "queendom" would be just as accurate. It is the title given to the lowest of the ten Qabbalistic spheres and corresponds to our mundane life circumstance.

This is the realm of normal, waking consciousness and of our day-to-day interactions with our physical environment. While its planetary symbol is the Earth, Malkuth is not our physical planet itself. Rather, it is the symbolic "zone girdling the Earth"; the lens through which all the cosmic forces represented by the higher spheres are focused directly into physical reality.

Malkuth is thus the interface between the purely astral energy matrix and the purely physical matter which naturally adheres to this matrix. This point of intersection is very dynamic.

Malkuth itself, is not a place that has physical, material density; but it is a place that has astral (emotional) and mental (essential meaning) density. Over the millennia, humans have pondered this astral realm and fashioned coherent symbols to express their findings.

The primary symbol that expresses the Malkuth interface of astral-matrix with physical-matter, is the division of all things, into Four Elements. This is depicted by the so called "Cross of Equated Forces".

Contrary to the common orientation of West= Water and North=Earth, in the symbolic space of Malkuth, Fire is the opposite of Water, and Air is the opposite of Earth. This shifts the Elemental correspondences from the common West=Water to West =Earth, and from the common North=Earth to North=Water. **Take careful note of this Malkuth orientation.**

The circle, divided into quadrants, provides

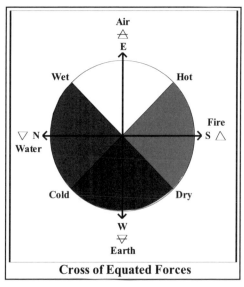

Cross of Equated Forces

the basic structure of Malkuth itself. Our Malkuth Temple however, is a square that encloses the central intersection of these four quadrants. When we enter the Malkuth Temple, we stand at the exact center of the Cross -- the point where the Four Elements are united in perfect balance.

Each side of the Temple is an archway that leads outward to that quarter's Elemental realm. Thus from within the Malkuth Temple, one can survey all four Elemental realms equally. Or one has the option of venturing out into the realms of the individual Elements.

The further details of the Malkuth Temple are designed to facilitate an exploration of this interface between astral-matrix and physical-matter. The medium of this exploration, is the language of symbols.

Since Malkuth is a symbolic space, our meditation will begin with a journey into the earth -- through a cave entrance and down a natural tunnel. This tunnel eventually leads to the Malkuth Temple.

The Malkuth Temple will be our permanent rendezvous point, so each meditation will begin with the same journey to the Malkuth Temple. With our first meditation, we will explore Malkuth; but in the 7 Temple meditations which follow in the series, we will be using the Malkuth Temple only as a launching point for our exploration of higher realms.

MEDITATION #1: MALKUTH

Reaching the Gateway

Find a private spot, where you are certain you will not be interrupted, and situate yourself comfortably. Thoroughly relax your body. Focus on the natural rhythm of your breathing and let go of all mundane concerns.

Close your eyes and visualize a cave entrance. A curtain is drawn across the entrance, bearing a specific symbol. Focus upon this symbol and picture it as clearly as you can.

Reaching Malkuth

Now speak (with your inner voice) the phrase: "Adonai (pronounced "ah-dough-nye"), please guide me to Malkuth."

In answer to your prayer, the Hebrew letters אדני (ADNI) appear near the top of the curtain, as if written with light. The upward pointing white triangle shines forth, as does the lowest of the ten spheres, and a soft light glows within the cave.

When you see this illumination, draw the curtain aside and enter the cave.

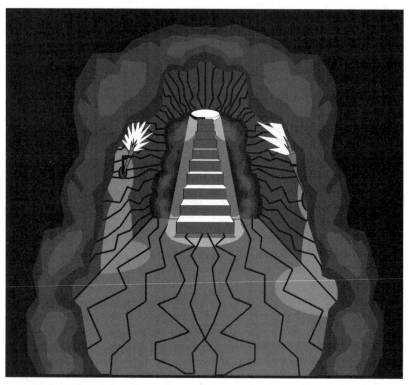

Before you stretches a rugged tunnel, hewn by natural forces through the dark bedrock. It is ten feet wide and as many tall, and extends for 30 paces. Before you proceed, take careful note of its features and build a stable image.

Ten paces in, you come to a torch mounted on the tunnel wall to your right. Pause here and examine the torch. Try to perceive it with all your senses: see it, hear it, smell it, feel its heat. Before continuing on, look around and reaffirm your visualization of the Tunnel from your current position.

Another ten paces in and there is a torch mounted on the left wall. Examine this torch as you did the first and similarly reorient your visualization of the Tunnel's interior.

Another ten paces in and you come to a steep stairway that leads directly upward through a perfectly circular opening in the tunnel roof. Light pours down the steps from the circular opening above. There are ten steps -- count them off to yourself as you climb.

When you reach the top of the stairs, you stand in the Malkuth Temple, facing toward the eastern quarter. I stand in the southeast corner (ahead, to the right), awaiting your arrival. [I'm a slender 5'11" tall, have wavy red hair, and sport a short red-and-grey beard. I'll be wearing a simple white ritual robe, cinctured with a blue-and-red belt, and over this, a red, floor length vestment.]

The Temple is built of hewn stone, the floor is translucent marble. At each quarter there sits a low altar, upon which burn two candles. Behind the quarter altars, veiling each archway, hang curtains made of gossamer silk.

Spend a few moments orienting yourself to the Malkuth Temple.

At the appropriate moment, I will gather the participants together and cast a ritual circle. I will then lead the participants clockwise around the circle, evoking each of the quarter Guardians, introducing the participants personally to each Guardian, and briefly exploring each of the Elemental realms.

The first realm we will explore is that of the Eastern quarter and the Element Air.

The Guardian of the Element is the archangel Raphael. In Hebrew, Raphael means "whom God heals". The healing that Raphael conveys is that of balance -- the essence of the Element Air.

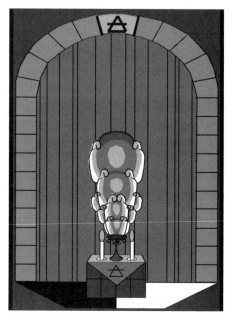

I light the incense upon the altar and say a few words. As I evoke Raphael's presence, the silk curtain disintegrates and then resolidifies in the image of Raphael. [Dressed in white, with white wings and a blaze of golden hair. The rising sun hangs on her/his breast.]

I introduce each participant to Raphael. The archangel greets each and shares a few private words.

Next we turn to the realm of Air which lies behind Raphael and stretches as far as the eye can see. We step together through the archway into this realm for a brief exploration . . .

Air is the joining and blending of the opposite qualities of Fire and Water. It is said to combine Fire's heat with Water's moisture, but to say that Air is "warm and moist" is an overstatement. Air, in fact, is not "warm"; rather, it is "neither cold nor hot". For in Air, hot and cold (expansion and contraction) cancel each other out, resulting in a "temperate" neutrality. In comparison to Water, Air is warm; but when compared to Fire, it is cold. Likewise, Air is not "moist" per se; rather, it is a middle ground between sopping wet Water and bone dry Fire.

This mediating, synthesizing nature is the essence of the Element Air. It is "weightlessness", mediating between the downward gravity of Water and the upward urgency of Fire. It is the straight line, tending neither upward nor downward *of its own accord.*

This brings us to another prime aspect of Air -- its mutability. While Air has no bias of its own, it readily accepts the impress of any force it encounters. For this reason, the rational aspects of the human mind are associated with Air.

The factor of Air's mutability combined with its tendency toward mediation or balance, establishes Air as the symbol for all communications. Human speech, writing, etc., all fall under the domain of this Element.

The anthropomorphic representations, or so called "beings of the Element", of Air are the Sylphs. These are usually seen as very small, elusive humanoids, possessing translucent wings. The Sylphs inhabit what is usually seen as a vast misty region, with areas of pristine clarity and other areas of murky obscurity.

I say "usually seen as" here because these symbols are not universal. For the most part they are cultural; but even within a single culture, these symbols are clothed with infinite variety. Symbols are ultimately personal, intimate things. No two of us will experience a symbol in exactly the same way. A symbol, by its very nature, is an interaction -- between the thing symbolized and the being perceiving the symbol.

It is important to honor the essential uniqueness of our perceptions. We each see things in our own unique way. So if you don't see little flying creatures, don't worry. Perhaps you are perceiving the Sylphs as thoughts which gently brush against your awareness, or as some other symbol more relevant to your personal experience and temperament. This is simply Nature's way.

FURTHER CORRESPONDENCES: **Positive Principle:** Mediating, communicating. **Negative Principle:** Ungrounding, dispersing. **Bodily Sense:** Smell. **Astral Sense:** Clairaudience. **Body Part:** Chest. **Color & Shape:** Yellow Crescent. **Tarot:** Swords, Knights. **Misc. Symbols:** Incense; feather; sword; sunrise; all things gaseous. **Temperament = Sanguine:** (+) Optimism, penetration, joy, diligence, kindness, independence. (-) Contempt, slyness, dishonesty.

←——————————————→

. . . When we are done, we return to the archway (it is always directly behind you -- simply turn around and there it is) and pass back into the Malkuth Temple. We thank Raphael for his/her hospitality and pass clockwise around the Temple.

The second realm we encounter is that of the Southern quarter and the Element Fire.

The Guardian of the Element is the archangel Mikael. In Hebrew, Mikael means "made in the image of God". The image that Mikael presents is one of radiant power -- the essence of the Element Fire.

I light the flame upon the altar and say a few words. As I evoke the Guardian's presence, the silk curtain disintegrates and then re-solidifies in the image of Mikael. [Dressed in scarlet red, with flaming wings and bright red hair. His whole appearance flames.]

I introduce each participant to Mikael. The archangel greets each and shares a few private words.

Next we turn to the realm of Fire which lies behind Mikael and stretches as far as the eye can see. We step together through the archway into this realm for a brief exploration . . .

Fire is the archetypal symbol for radiant energy. It causes expansion, an upward and outward movement, and excitation, in whatever it encounters. It also consumes whatever it touches; or rather, it transforms whatever it touches into a higher state of being.

Fire is electric, hot and dry. It symbolizes the divine and the human will, strength, power and passion. Its effects range from the changeably severe, to the steadily nurturing. At whatever level one encounters it, Fire is always active, and always communicates its heat to its surroundings.

The "beings" of Fire are called Salamanders, and are usually described as having a reptilian appearance. This stems from the angular nature of Fire which tends to manifest symbolically in elongated salamander-like shapes. The Salamanders inhabit what is usually seen as an exciting realm of dancing flames, erupting volcanoes, and so on.

FURTHER CORRESPONDENCES: **Positive Principle:** Energizing, empowering. **Negative Principle:** Consuming, burning. **Bodily Sense:** Sight. **Astral Sense:** Clairvoyance. **Body Part:** Head. **Color & Shape:** Red Triangle. **Tarot:** Wands, Kings. **Misc. Symbols:** Flame; red candle; wand; high noon. **Temperament = Choleric:** (+) Courage, enthusiasm, resolution. (-) Gluttony, jealousy, irritability, destructiveness.

← ⎯⎯⎯⎯⎯⎯⎯⎯⎯⎯⎯⎯→

. . . When we are done, we return to the archway and pass back into the Malkuth Temple. We thank Mikael for his hospitality and pass clockwise around the Temple.

The third realm we encounter is that of the Western quarter and the Element Earth.

The Guardian of the Element is the archangel Gabriel. In Hebrew, Gabriel means "whom God made strong". The strength Gabriel possesses is the power of so-lidification -- the essence of the Element Earth.

I speak a few words and the great crystal upon the West altar shines forth with an inner radiance. As I evoke the Guardian's presence, the silk curtain disintegrates and then re-solidifies in the image of Gabriel. [Dressed in dark browns and greens, with black wings and jet black hair. Her/his wings are not for flight, but for enclosing us in a gracious hug of greeting.]

I introduce each participant to Gabriel. The archangel greets each and shares a few private words.

Next we turn to the realm of Earth which lies behind Gabriel and stretches as far as the eye can see. We step through the archway into this realm for a brief exploration . . .

23

← —————————————————————— →

Earth is the opposite of Air. Where Air is weightlessness, Earth is weightiness. Where Air mediates between opposing influences, Earth takes those influences to their extremes of manifestation. Earth is coalescing, solidifying, crystallizing, grounding. It is the foundation from which Fire moves upward, toward which Water descends, and over which Air hovers.

Part of the mystery of this Element is that it does not exist in and of itself. Which is to say, it is the product of the interaction between Fire, Air and Water: When Fire meets Water, Air results. When Fire and Water then interact through this medium of Air, the *three-part interaction* is called Earth. The positive Fire and the negative Water unite to form the neutral Air; together they form the dynamic positive-neutral-negative electro-magnetism of Earth.

Some say that Earth is not a "true" Element, but this is a fine point of philosophy and consequently not of much importance to practical experience. In practice, Earth is every bit as much an Element as Fire or Water.

Our overall consciousness itself (seen as a conglomeration of various Fiery, Airy and Watery aspects brought to singular manifestation) and the physical organism which houses it, are both attributed to Earth. As are all things heavy and solid.

The words solid and stocky, best describe the "beings" of Earth, called Gnomes. They are usually seen as short, thick, dark, bearded, clothed in simple utilitarian garb, and very friendly to humans. Their realm is subterranean and they happily enact all of Nature's underground mysteries.

FURTHER CORRESPONDENCES: **Positive Principle:** Grounding, solidifying. **Negative Principle:** Blocking, halting, obscuring. **Bodily Sense:** Taste. **Astral Sense:** Clairsentience. **Body Part:** Legs, bones, flesh. **Color & Shape:** Black Square. **Tarot:** Disks, Princess'. **Misc. Symbols:** Dirt; salt; cornucopia; pentacle; sunset. **Temperament = Phlegmatic:** (+) Endurance, consideration, punctuality, responsibility, objectivity. (-) Unreliability, unscrupulousness, dullness, laziness.

← —————————————————————— →

. . . When we are done, we return to the archway and pass back into the Malkuth Temple. We thank Gabriel for his/her hospitality and pass clockwise around the Temple.

The fourth and final realm we encounter is that of the Northern quarter and the Element Water.

The Guardian of this Element is the archangel Haniel. In Hebrew, Haniel means "whom God made gracious". Haniel expresses her grace as a magnetic fluidity -- the essence of the Element Water.

I speak a few words over the Water chalice sitting upon the altar, and a beautiful rainbow suddenly appears. As I evoke the Guardian's presence, the silk curtain disintegrates and then re-solidifies in the image of Haniel. [Dressed in flowing bright blues and watery greens, with seafoam wings and seaweed brown hair. Her embrace feels cleansing, as if a refreshing current of water has passed through one's entire body from head to foot.]

I introduce each participant to Haniel. The archangel greets each and shares a few private words.

Next we turn to the realm of Water which lies behind Haniel and stretches as far as the eye can see. We step through the archway into this realm for a brief exploration . . .

Water is the polar opposite of Fire. It is cold, wet, constrictive, magnetic , and downward tending. Where Fire is angular, Water is curvilinear and fluid. Where Fire is brute force of will, Water is the undeniable force of emotion, feeling and intuition, and of persistent effort. Fire cleanses by burning-away: Water cleanses by washing-away. Fire nurtures by exciting things to life: Water nurtures by calming things to a sustainable rhythm..

The Element Water is the archetypal ocean, mother of all life. She is filled with potentialities, each pursuing their own path toward manifestation. It is a beautiful and alluring realm, populated by "beings" called Undines. These creatures are usually seen as half fish or dol-

25

phin, and half human. Usually the upper half is human, symbolizing the evolution from primal-form into final-form. They speak the language of emotions and communicate beauty in their form and actions. They symbolize all of Nature's watery ways.

FURTHER CORRESPONDENCES: **Positive Principle:** Healing, creating, flowing. **Negative Principle:** De-stabilizing, constricting. **Bodily Sense:** Hearing. **Astral Sense:** Clairfeeling. **Body Part:** Abdomen. **Color & Shape:** Blue Circle. **Tarot:** Cups, Queens. **Misc. Symbols:** All liquids; chalice; seashells; midnight. **Temperament = Melancholic:** (+) Compassion, respectability, modesty, calmness, devotion. (-) Shyness, indifference, depression.

$$\longleftarrow\joinrel\longrightarrow$$

. . . When we are done, we return to the archway and pass back into the Malkuth Temple. We thank Haniel for her hospitality and pass clockwise, returning to the Eastern quarter.

When the astral ritual is complete and we have explored each of the Elemental realms, I will release the circle casting. Participants will then exit the way they came: down the stairs, along the tunnel, out the cave entrance, ultimately returning to normal physical awareness.

Follow-up Work

Immediately write down a few notes outlining the key points of your experience. This will help bring your more ephemeral astral experiences, firmly into the grasp of your normal waking consciousness. It will also greatly facilitate the integration of those experiences into your daily life.

In the days immediately following your Malkuth meditation, focus your attention upon perceiving the Four Elements as they manifest in the world around you and within you. As you notice the things in your environment, analyze them and try to discern their Elemental composition. What Element predominates in this or that thing? How are the other, less predominant, Elements manifest?

Don't be too rigid in your analysis. Remember that all things exist in combination. What seems at first glance to be pure Fire for example, is in reality a combination of all four Elements. They must all four be present for physical manifestation to occur.

Likewise analyze your interactions with other people. What Element predominates in your exchange? How are the other Elements manifest?

And finally, turn this analysis inward and examine your internal world of mental and emotional responses to the outer world. What Element predominates in the personality you manifest? How are the other Elements manifest? Again, I caution against being too rigid in your analysis.

Return regularly to the Malkuth Temple and pursue a further, more thorough exploration of the Elemental realms. Explore not only their external, universal meaning and significance, but also search out their internal, personal meaning. In other words, use the Elements to connect your internal world with your experience of the external universe. The Elements can be a handy tool for understanding the inner and outer worlds, and a powerful tool for effectively uniting these all-too-often disparate realms.

As you become more familiar with each of the Four Elements, focus your efforts upon the personality you manifest. Examine your personality closely and analyze it with the tool of the Four Elements. Determine which parts of it correspond with which of the Elemental influences, and in this way, thoroughly catalogue the personality you currently manifest. Do not, at this point, engage in changing your personality -- for now, you are only to catalogue it and come to know its current parameters.

While working in the Malkuth Temple, be sure to carefully cultivate your friendship with the Quarter Guardians. Treat them always with kindness, respect and with absolute honesty, and they will become true friends.

Introduction

Yesod (pronounced "yes-odd") is generally translated into English as "foundation". Other uses of the word encompass the ideas of secrecy, consultation and assembly.

The realm of Yesod is the hidden pattern to which matter adheres. In Malkuth we witnessed the dynamic point of interface between this underlying energy matrix and physical matter. Here in Yesod though, we encounter the energy matrix itself.

In very universal terms, this energy matrix is the intermediary state between mind and matter. If we symbolically posit mind as a gaseous state and matter as a solid state, then the astral matrix is seen as an intermediate, liquid state which shares features of both. Thus the astral substance is shaped by mind and in turn, determines the shape of matter.

The astral substance itself is caused by the passage of universal-mind into specific-matter and exists only because of this passage. As individual-minds pass through the astral substance, the astral crystallizes, forming an energy matrix to which matter invariably adheres. This is rightly called an "astral body" in that it is an organic structure through which individual-mind becomes active within the astral realm, and by extension, within the physical realm. Every material thing is founded upon an astral body.

The moment mind releases itself from matter, the corresponding astral matrix begins to decay. This happens because there is no longer a flow of mind through the astral substance and therefore, no longer a mental-matrix in place to determine and sustain the astral crystallization.

During material incarnation, individual-mind (whether it be manifest as a human being, a rock, a tree, or a bird does not matter) is invariably provided with experiences which cause it to evolve and mature. As individual-mind is changed by its incarnation, those changes will be reflected in the crystallization of the astral substance (and to a lesser extent, they will be reflected in the crystallization of the material substance or physical body).

All of these universal aspects of the astral substance become easier to comprehend when we consider our own human manifestation of them. Indeed, personalizing one's experience of the astral is the first step in learning how to work effectively with its more universal manifestations. Thus, our focus in this meditation will be upon how Yesod manifests within each of us individually.

In directly human terms, Yesod is the personality we manifest -- that unique combination of habits, idiosyncrasies, preferences, and countless other factors, through which we express our inner selves, externally. Generally, our personalities are not clear reflections of our inner selves, but rather a compromise between the demands of our inner and outer worlds.

Boiled down to its most basic elements, each personality contains aspects that are sub-consciously motivated; others that are consciously intended; and still others that flow from super-conscious levels. This points out an inherent three-fold nature of the personality, and the astral substance in general, symbolized almost universally by the three faces of the "triple-goddess": maiden, mother and crone.

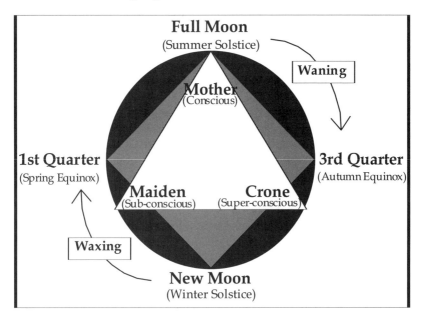

Astrologically, the astral matrix is symbolized by the Moon with her three faces: waxing crescent, full moon and waning crescent. The Moon takes in the Sun's light (just as the astral matrix accepts the mental influx) and then reflects it to Earth (just as the astral matrix reflects the mental impress onto matter). But the Moon, like the astral body, not only takes in the Sun's light, it also changes it once it's been absorbed. Thus the light eventually reflected to Earth, has been altered. In symbolic terms, it has been tuned by the Moon to a non-solar rhythm -- which is to say, it's been personalized.

During the span of one solar year (the time it takes the Sun to circle the zodiac), the Moon will accomplish the same task 13 times. The Moon moves around the entire zodiac (the equivalent of a solar year) in approximately 28 days, making it the fastest and most versatile of the planets. It constantly passes into, and quickly out of, aspect with each of the other planets; and just like the personality, it weaves together all the various planetary influences.

The 13x12 rhythm of the Moon interlocks the 1x12 rhythm of the Sun, with the 1x4 rhythm of the Earth, through its 3-faces (waxing, full and waning). The lunation cycle mimics both the 4 seasons of the Earth and the 12 zodiacal periods of the sun as it passes through its four-phases (new, first quarter, full and last quarter). A lunation (passage from one new moon to the next new moon; a.k.a. "moonth" or "month") is longer than a single lunar circling of the zodiac. Since the lunation is a geo-soli-lunar cycle, the concurrent movement of the Sun means that the Moon passes through 13 signs of the zodiac from one new moon (conjunction of moon and sun) to the next new moon, resulting in 12 lunations per solar-year (13x12 = 12x13).

Sound complex? Well, it is and this perfectly reflects the complexity of the human personality! But just because a thing is complex, doesn't mean that there are no simple ways by which to gain an understanding of it.

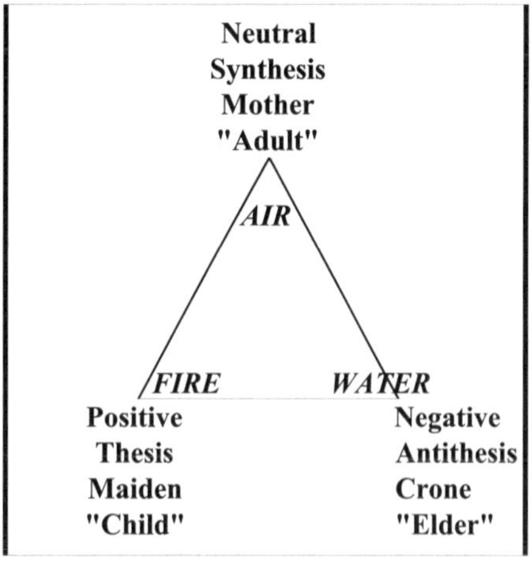

Earlier I stated that the element Earth is really the result of the interaction of Fire, Air and Water. In Yesod, we are confronted with this three-fold interaction itself and not with the resultant Earth as we were in Malkuth. Therefore the symbol of the triangle is where we will start in our path to understanding Yesod.

Yesod represents fluidity, periodicity and reflection. Just as the four Elements of

Neutral
Synthesis
Mother
"Adult"

AIR

FIRE   WATER
Positive   Negative
Thesis   Antithesis
Maiden   Crone
"Child"   "Elder"

Malkuth are self-multiplied resulting in the 16 sub-Elements, so also the three faces of Yesod are self-multiplied and result in 9 aspects.

The following figure is one example of how the personality can be analyzed into 9 aspects. This particular approach is, on the one hand,

33

simple enough to work with, while on the other hand, it's confusing enough to sufficiently represent the complexities of the human personality!

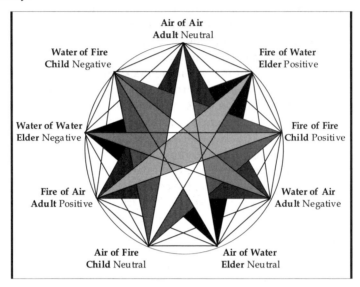

Though its complexity might seem a disadvantage, it is nonetheless intentional. It forces us to use more than just our rational minds to reach an understanding of it -- we must also intuit the relationships and dynamics it illustrates.

Yesod is seen as the combination (assembly) of Tiphareth/Sun (mental matrix), Netzach/Venus (lower instinctual emotions), and Hod/Mercury (lower rational intellect). As such, it is a realm that is unlocked only when we employ ration in conjunction with emotion. Approaching it only rationally will not get one any further than approaching it only emotionally -- either course will lead one to an incomplete experience of this realm.

In the Malkuth meditation, I spoke of analyzing your personality with the tool of the Four Elements. In Yesod, we see those Elemental aspects of personality in action. Here they are joined as complexes. Each of the nine faces of Yesod (e.g., ADULT Neutral, CHILD Negative, etc.) represents a complex of several Elemental aspects, working together in unison. So in Yesod, we can reach into the most dynamic manifestation of these Elemental factors.

The titles of these nine aspects are meant to be very general descriptions of very personal things. For example, the CHILD

Negative station is one we will all easily recognize. It is typified by our urge to throw a tantrum when we don't get our way. While this is an aspect of self we all manifest, it is manifest uniquely by each one of us. My own CHILD Negative is a complex of specific Elemental influences -- your own CHILD Negative is a similar complex, but composed of a slightly different set of Elemental influences.

The average human manifests a personality that is primarily emotional, reactionary and sub-consciously motivated (i.e., instinctual). We have all experienced this way of being: shaped by circumstances and adrift with little true self-determination.

Yet, hidden within the foundation of the personality, are assembled all the tools for self-crafting a conscious personality, one which clearly reflects the individual-mind's influx. Since self-crafting of one's own personality is, as I said before, the first step in learning to work with the more universal facets of the astral substance, our task in this meditation will be to familiarize ourselves with the intricacies of our personalities as they are reflected to us in the Yesod Temple.

The Temple itself has nine sides, each of which reflects one of the nine aspects of the personality.

At each station, you will find a mirror, seated upon a throne. The mirror symbolizes the Moon's reflectivity and the fact that the passage of sunlight is what drives the whole process. The throne has a square seat and four legs, symbolizing the four Elements. The square platform the throne sits upon, symbolizes the material manifestation of this enthroned personality-aspect.

The upright back of the throne, mixes the mirror's curvature and the Elemental squareness below it. It is surmounted by three phases of the Moon which symbolize the progression of the influxing sunlight: from Super-conscious (Dark Moon) to Sub-conscious (waxing Quarter Moon) to Conscious (Full Moon).

Behind the throne, forming a part of the Temple structure itself, stands an archway supported by two pillars. The white pillar symbolizes the polarity of force, and the black symbolizes that of form. The arch which surmounts and unites these poles, is composed of 28 stones -- one for each of the days it takes the Moon to circle the zodiac. [These are known as the 28 "mansions of the Moon".] This archway opens to the star-filled infinity of deep space, symbolizing the universal-mind's influx (each star an individual-mind) from higher levels which sustains the astral matrix.

Though illustrated here in only black-and-white tones (pretty much all that's visible on a moonlit night), the ray of light that strikes the mirror is in reality tinged with color. That ray starts as sunlight, but during its passage through Yesod, it is shifted to the spectrum of reflected light (i.e., the pigment colors). The example illustrated above, is meant to be the "ADULT Neutral" face, so the ray of sunlight might reflect from the mirror as a bright, pure yellow.

MEDITATION #2: YESOD

Begin as in the Malkuth Meditation: pass through the Cave Entrance, along the Tunnel passage, up the ten steps, and into the Malkuth Temple where I stand awaiting your arrival.

When all the participants have arrived, I will gather us together and cast a ritual circle.

Once our circle is cast, we will spend several moments together in the center of the Malkuth Temple, holding hands in a circle and bringing our awareness of the presences of the other participants into focus. As you look around the circle, try to sense the unique presence of each participant. Look to your own uniqueness and honor the differences and similarities you perceive in the others.

At the appropriate moment, I will bring our focus to the East quarter altar -- our gateway to Yesod. Upon the altar there now sits a mirror and behind it we see the same curtain and symbol we encounter at the Cave Entrance.

As I light the candles upon the altar, we each see our own face reflected back to us from the mirror. Then together, as with a single voice, we speak the phrase: "Shaddai (pronounced "shuh-dye"), please guide me to Yesod."

In answer to our prayer, the Hebrew letters שׁדי (ShDI) appear near the top of the curtain, as if written with light. The upward pointing white triangle shines forth, as does

37

the next-to-lowest of the ten spheres, and a soft light glows behind the curtain.

When we see this illumination, I reach forward and draw the curtain aside. Hand-in-hand, we all pass through the archway. We are immediately greeted by a flash of lightning and a resounding boom of thunder.

Our transition to the Yesod Temple is sudden and complete. We stand, holding hands, at the center of the nine-pointed star mosaic.

Take a few moments to visually orient yourself to the Yesod Temple; and at the same time, notice the presences of the other participants and your hand-held connection to them.

At the appropriate moment, I will bring our focus together and we will then release the hands we have been holding. I will direct each of you individually to the very center of the Yesod Temple and ask you to call out your name. [Note: This will happen for you all individually and simultaneously, so you needn't visualize yourself having to stand in line, awaiting your turn, etc.]

As you speak your name, the Temple darkens and your awareness of the other participants disappears. Suddenly, a ray of bright sunlight descends from directly above you and strikes the crown of your head. It passes down and into you, then bursts forth from your heart center as nine differently colored rays. Each one of these rays reaches out and strikes one of the nine darkened mirrors, illuminating them all with your own refection.

These are the nine faces of your own unique personality. Take your time now to investigate the image reflected in each of the nine mirrors. I recommend that for your first experience of Yesod, you work your way clockwise around the Temple and focus primarily upon identifying each of these aspects of yourself. You will naturally be tempted to deny certain parts of yourself and to embrace others, but I urge you to avoid this sort of judgmentalism for the moment and adopt a more objective attitude. You can always return to the Yesod Temple and pursue a more thorough self-examination later. For now, your objective is to begin the process by learning to recognize the faces of your personality.

If you encounter something that either frightens you so much that you feel yourself needing to escape, or pleases you so much that you find yourself entranced, immediately distance yourself from it. Take note of it and identify it, but nonetheless distance yourself from it. Approach your first encounter with Yesod systematically and without any dallying.

At the appropriate time, I will call everyone away from their private explorations and back to a group focus at the center of the Yesod Temple. We will take a moment to again join hands and to notice the presences of the other participants.

Then together, as with a single voice, we speak the word "Malkuth" and we find ourselves suddenly transiting back through the archway into the Malkuth Temple. Again we stand together in the center of the Malkuth Temple, holding hands in a circle.

After a few moments of re-orientation, I will release the circle casting. Participants will then exit the way they came: down the stairs, along the Tunnel, and out the Cave Entrance, ultimately returning to normal physical awareness.

Follow-up Work

As before, immediately write down a few notes outlining the key points of your experience.

Then try to remember each of the nine faces you saw and write a brief description of the ones you recall. This particular information should not be shared with anyone else -- the exploration of your personality is to be conducted in privacy. This will foster a sense of security and will aid you in your work with your personality by providing you a safe space within which to exercise the radical self-honesty such work will require of you.

In the days immediately following your Yesod meditation, take note of the faces you recognized as they show themselves in your actions. At different points during this time, something you say or do will remind you clearly of one of the faces you saw during the meditation. Take a mental note when this occurs and compare the real-life manifestation with the remembered face. In this way, you will experience connection between the Yesodic symbol and the material reality.

Return regularly to the Yesod Temple and thoroughly familiarize yourself with each of the nine faces mirrored there. Work your way carefully past/through your natural self-judgmentalism till you come to a place of self-acceptance and self-love.

This place of self-acceptance is a "place of great power". From this dynamic place you can begin to safely and effectively change the personality you see manifest. When you can stand in the center of the Yesod Temple, stare each mirror in the face, and accept with love everything you see as the raw material you must work with, then you are certainly ready to begin self-crafting.

In the Yesod Temple, I advise that you support your self-crafting efforts by visualizing appropriately symbolic tools. For example, when I work with self-crafting my personality in Yesod, I envision a simple throne stationed at the exact center of the Temple. I sit myself down in the throne and speak my name. As the ray of sunlight descends into me, I accept conscious control of it. I then turn my throne (it's on a lazy-susan sort of thing I guess) to the aspect/mirror of my choosing and consciously emit the ray that emerges from my heart center. I look at the reflection, ask myself how clearly it reflects the incoming light, and decide the ways in which I desire to change it. I visualize these changes occurring and I take very, very careful note of what actions are required to manifest these changes in my day-to-day life.

Please take note here: As I stated earlier, the astral is crystallized only by the passage of mind into specific-matter. Modification of the astral crystallization (i.e., astral-body/personality) can only be accomplished if specific changes are brought all the way down into material manifestation. In other words, visualization alone (i.e., bringing the mental down into the astral) does not suffice to effect genuine change in your personality. You must consciously integrate those intended changes into your daily life (i.e., bring the astra-mental down into the material). Otherwise they will remain only aspirations, never becoming fully permanent, reliable aspects of your manifest personality.

The goal of Yesodic self-crafting is to consciously crystallize the astral substance -- to manifest a personality that clearly reflects the individual mental influx. Yup, that is a never ending, lifelong process! It is also the conscious use of Nature's own ways, so we are always supported by the universe in such work.

Hod

Introduction

Hod (pronounced either "hawd" or "hoad") translates into English as "splendor; glory; majesty; beauty; and, brightness". To this realm is attributed the bright, rapidly moving, hermaphroditic planet Mercury. Astrologically, Mercury symbolizes communication of all kinds, rational thought, and all systems dependent upon communication between one part and another (bodies, machines, organizations, philosophies, etc.).

In universal terms, as mind descends through the astral substance, it polarizes into force and form. These poles are symbolized by the planets Mercury (form) and Venus (force). [At a higher mental level, these same poles are symbolized by Mars (form) and Jupiter (force).]

In human terms, our emotions are the force represented by Venus. Indeed, it is in Netzach that we will explore all the emotional archetypes.

Our ability to reason and tie things together into logical order is the form symbolized by Mercury. And here in the Hod meditation we will be exploring Paul Case's statement, "#8: I look forward with confidence to the perfect realization of the eternal Splendor of the Limitless Light." [From his "Pattern on the Trestleboard."]

Mercury represents our penetrating ability to connect one detail, one train of thought, etc., with another. Again in universal terms, it represents the descending mind organizing the raw Venusian force. This organization results in the intricate complexity we easily observe in the universe -- as well as in the infinite complexity of our ability to observe complex things.

After polarizing, the descending mind rejoins the poles of force and form in Yesod. In human terms then, our personalities (Yesod) are a combination of emotion (Netzach / Venus / force) and rationality (Hod / Mercury / form).

The Qabbalistic Tree of Life image provides one of the better illustrations of this:

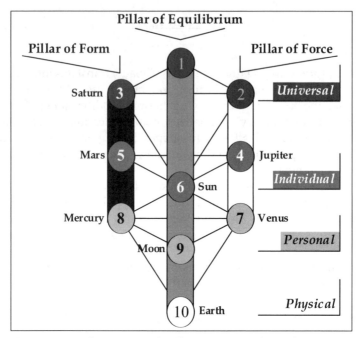

Here we see three vertical pillars: two are the polar extremes of force and form; and one equilibrates between them.

There are also four horizontal levels: universal (1, 2, & 3); individual (4, 5, & 6); personal (7, 8, & 9); and physical (10).

Following the numerical order of the spheres illustrates the descent of the Unity into the plurality of matter. As the universal descends into the individual level, it polarizes to right (4), then left (5), and then equilibrates (6). The same is true as the individual descends into the personal realm -- it polarizes to the right (7 / Venus / emotions / force), then to the left (8 / Mercury / rationality / form), and then balances those two in Yesod (9 / Moon / personality).

In this series of meditations, we're following the reverse-numerical order and working our way up the diagram. Thus far, our Temples have been stationed along the pillar of equilibrium, but now we are straying to the left hand pole of form.

It's important to keep in mind that Hod is polarized, for to experience the whole of Hod we must bring to it a balanced understanding of our personalities. Without that balance, it is easy to get lost in the minutia of Hod's complexity and conclude that the universe is a strictly rational thing after all. Likewise with Netzach -- without a balanced approach, it is easy to be swept away by the primal emotions encountered there and conclude that the universe is completely irrational after all. Both of these polarized perspectives are correct and at the same time incorrect. Only when joined together do they accurately know that the universe is both rational and irrational.

The Hod Temple is known as the "Library of Hermes". This library has eight (the number of Mercury) sides and is six (the number of the Sun) stories tall. Each of the solar-six levels have 12 (the number of the zodiac) arched doorways paired with 12 bookcases. Conversely, each of the mercurial-eight sides have nine (the number of the Moon) archways and bookcases. There are thus 72 (6x12 = 8x9 = 72) archways with corresponding bookcases in total. [This illustrates the Qabbalistic "72-fold Name of God" which, due to its overwhelming complexity, I won't elucidate here.]

The intention is to symbolize that all of human thought is gathered here in the library of Hermes. Each archway leads to a chamber in which you can explore a rational understanding of a specific aspect of the universe's complexity. The bookcase to the left, abutting the black pillar of each archway, is filled with books relating to that archway's explorable subject matter.

With familiarity, this library can become a busy, alive place for you. Within each chamber you will find students and teachers pursuing a specific subject. There is even a librarian who will help you find your way around!

I say "with familiarity" because it usually takes several exploratory visits before one connects with this level of Hod and accesses the guidance that comes with it. My first visits to Hermes' Library were solitary and somewhat confusing. I couldn't read the writing in any of the books and didn't encounter either students or teachers, let alone a librarian! Then one visit, I encountered a teacher and from that point on, my awareness of other presences rapidly increased.

For our introduction to the Hod Temple, we will be choosing a specific book from a specific bookcase and entering a specific archway. The book will contain Paul Case's statement, "#8: I look forward with confidence to the perfect realization of the eternal Splendor of the Limitless Light." Within the chamber, we will encounter a teacher who will lead us in a rational exploration of this statement's meaning.

This illustrates one way of working with the Hod Temple -- select a book, pass through the archway with it, and access a rational exploration of the book's topic. This works best if you know what book to choose and where to find it, but in the absence of this knowledge, this method can also be used to discover what an archway's subject matter might be. For instance, you could select a book at random, pass through the archway with it, and then try to read it while inside the chamber. Ask aloud for guidance and visualize the presence of a teacher to assist you.

An alternate approach, especially effective if you don't know where to find something, is to seek guidance as to where to find the archway and bookcase corresponding to your chosen subject matter. Simply stand in the center of the library and state your need. Listen for and then follow your intuition (this inner voice is the "librarian" I mentioned) and you will be guided to the correct archway and book.

You can also search the library by teacher, asking for guidance to a specific teacher instead of a specific subject matter.

Lastly, you can also just open yourself to the recommendations of Hod's inner guidance and ask "Elohim Tzabauth, what do I need to learn at this moment?" This can lead to some amazing experiences!

MEDITATION #3: HOD

Begin as before: pass through the Cave Entrance, along the Tunnel passage, up the ten steps, and into the Malkuth Temple where I stand awaiting your arrival.

When all the participants have arrived, I will gather us together and cast a ritual circle.

Once our circle is cast, we will spend several moments together in the center of the Malkuth Temple, holding hands in a circle and bringing our awareness of the presences of the other participants into focus. As you look around the circle, try to sense the unique presence of each participant.

At the appropriate moment, I will bring our focus to the East quarter altar -- our gateway to Hod.

Upon the altar there now sits a scroll and behind it we see the same curtain and symbol we encounter at the Cave Entrance.

Upon the scroll we see an eight-pointed figure (representing the complex mercurial expression of the solar influx) and, in Hebrew script, the god/dess name attributed to Hod.

I light the candles upon the altar, then together, as with a single voice, we speak the phrase: "Elohim Tzabauth (pronounced "e h - l o w - h e e m tzaw-baw-ooth"), please guide me to Hod."

In answer to our prayer, the He-

49

brew letters צבאות אלהים (ALHIM TzBAUTh) appear near the top of the curtain, as if written with light. The upward pointing white triangle shines forth, as does the lowest sphere on the left-hand pillar, and a soft light glows behind the curtain.

When we see this illumination, I reach forward and draw the curtain aside. Hand-in-hand, we all pass through the archway.

Our transition to the Hod Temple is gentle and causes no disorientation. We now stand, holding hands, at the center of the eight-pointed-star floor mosaic. We take a few moments to examine our surroundings . . .

At the appropriate moment, I will bring our focus together. Staying on the first floor level, we will then walk to the east wall of the Temple and extract a single book from the bookcase to the left of the archway. Together, we will step through the archway and enter the hidden chamber.

Here we find a low table upon which I place the book and then open it to a chosen page. Look closely at this page and do your best to read the printed words there. These words are Paul Case's statement -- "#8: I look forward with confidence to the perfect realization of the eternal Splendor of the Limitless Light."

After we have each read these printed words, I will call forth a teacher for us. Open yourself to perceiving this teacher in whatever way comes naturally to you. For some the teacher will be seen as a person you can converse with, but for others, this might manifest non-visually as a feeling, an intuition, as something you hear, or as a train of thoughts that just pops into your head.

Once the teacher arrives, we all sit down, holding hands in a circle, and silently meditate together upon the words we have read from the book. The teacher will enter into and lead our meditations. As I said, we may each perceive this somewhat differently so try to maintain an attitude of openness to whatever occurs naturally for you.

Feel free to probe and question and explore the various bits of information you access. We will spend several minutes with this meditation on statement #8, so there is no rush.

At the appropriate moment, I gather our focus together and we will thank our teacher for the lessons we've learned. I will gather up the book, lead us back out into the Hod Temple, and return the book to its case.

Then we will take a few minutes to walk around the whole Temple, making our way up to the sixth floor and back down. [The stairways connecting the floors are located on the west wall of the Temple and have not been illustrated in my east-facing graphic rendition.] Along the way, we will poke our heads into three different archways and take a brief moment to get an idea of what subject matter each one concerns.

When this exploration is complete, I will gather us together at the center of the floor mosaic. We will join hands and then together, as if with a single voice, we speak the word "Malkuth". This transits us gently back to the center of the Malkuth Temple.

After a few moments of re-orientation, I will release the circle casting. Participants will then exit the way they came: down the stairs, along the tunnel, and out the Cave entrance, ultimately returning to normal physical awareness.

Follow-up Work

Return regularly to the Hod Temple and use this asset to increase your (rational) understanding of things. Choose subjects which interest you and which are relevant to the self-crafting of your personality, and try pursuing them by yourself within the Hod Temple. As you refine your (rational) understanding, apply what you learn in Hod to your work in Yesod and Malkuth.

Explore each of Hod's six floors and familiarize yourself with the layout of the library. Use your imagination and discover also, the many different methods of accessing the information available in the Hod Temple.

Introduction

Netzach (pronounced "netz-awk", with a back-of-the-throat glottal "k" sound) translates into English variously as "truthfulness, uprightness, faithfulness"; "permanency, perpetuity, eternity"; "excellency, glory"; and, "completeness, entireness, perfection." Paul Case, adding these meanings together, translated it as "victorious life".

Taken as a string of hieroglyphs, the Hebrew word 'Nun-Tzaddi-Cheth' combines the image of abundance (Nun="fish"), with that of self-nurturance (Tzaddi="fishhook") and that of the personalized life force (Cheth="fence"). Thus Netzach (the realm of Venus) is seen as the embodiment of the abundant, self-nurturing life force -- with the emphasis on force.

This force cannot be defined rationally. It cannot be dissected with logic, written down, and communicated with exactitude from one person to another. There is no second-hand, intellectual way of grasping this force -- though in Hod, we could understand its form through ration -- this force can only be understood by experiencing it directly for oneself.

In human terms, Netzach is the realm of personal emotions. Or rather, it is the realm wherein the universal emotional archetypes intersect with personal expression. This intersection is pre-rational. It happens at an immediate, spontaneous, illogical, experiential level. It happens so quickly, there is no time for ration to interject itself. Ration can only intercede after the fact.

For example, when we encounter something, our first reaction is at an emotional gut level. It is immediate and spontaneous and we have no conscious control over it. Our ration then takes over and modifies the primary emotional response, crafting it into a more personal form. Generally, our ration focuses not on the something we've encountered in and of itself, but upon the force of our own primary response. Another way of putting it would be to say that the primary emotional response is the force which, generally, ignites the ration to action. The action of ration being the giving of form to emotion.

Netzach is the realm of the force of Nature; Hod, the realm of Nature's form. With logic we can understand her form, but logic fails us when we turn it toward the Mystery of her essential force. The Mystery cannot be grasped intellectually, it can only be experienced at a gut level. Our Netzach Temple is that gut level.

The Mystery is attributed to the number 7. Of the eight planetary numbers (3 through 10), seven is the only one which does not divide the 360 degrees of a circle with exactness. 360 divided by 7 equals 51.42857142857, with the last six digits repeating ad infinitum. This means that a circle cannot ever be divided into seven exactly equal parts. To draw a seven sided figure requires inexactitude, one has to estimate and judge by how it looks, and eventually let go of rational exactness.

Hidden in this Mystery of 7 into 360, is the meaning of the primary manifestation of dimensional time-space: the point. The point precedes the line. It has no other dimension than its singularity. It is both infinitely small and infinitely large. If we follow the point towards its smallness, we encounter an experience similar to dividing 360 by 7 -- since it is infinitely small by virtue of the infinity external to it, and infinitely large by virtue of the infinity within it, we find that it encompasses an infinite smallness which would take an infinite amount of time and effort for us to define.

It is not till we posit a second point and draw a line between them, that we are able to give the point real definition. Essentially, definition is a contextual illusion built upon the observable relationship of individually un-definable components.

Only through relationship is definition given to the point. And such is the case with the force of Netzach: only through personalization is it clothed in manifest form.

Love, loving-kindness, mercy: this is the primary force, at least in human terms. It is the dynamism of the point which, in its singularity, both encompasses infinity and is simultaneously encompassed. Thus we associate the goddess Venus with this realm, for here she is taken as the archetype of the human understanding of love.

This force of love itself has no opposite. It is only in the transition into form provided by the intercession of ration, that negative manifestations of this force occur. And these are found only in the humanoid heart and mind. In the rest of Nature, in the realm where specifically humanoid ration does not hold sway, the love force manifests without negatively polarized form.

This is due to the nature of different kinds of ration. For example, the type of ration encompassed by a tree or a rock as it gives form to the force of Nature, does not allow said rock or tree to express that force as mean-spiritedness. Human ration however, does allow such an expression -- it alone can divert or block the flow of love with as much ease as it can let love flow unhindered. A tree's ration does not encompass this power to divert and block, so it has no power to do anything but express the flow unhindered. But either result, be it human or tree, represents the giving of unique personal form to the same essential force.

While love itself does not have an opposite, it does, so to speak, have brothers and sisters. So in this realm of Netzach we encounter not only the primary force represented by Venus, but also all of the other archetypes of humanoid emotion. Here also are Mars, Phoebe, Jupiter, Artemis, Saturn, Astarte, Faunus, Pan, Kali, etc. Indeed, all the mythological expressions of human emotions can be found in Netzach, though generally, one meets the archetypes one is culturally most familiar with. This is another example of the 7 into 360 Mystery -- of the infinite diversity of uniqueness that is naturally manifest as force takes form.

Our Netzach Temple is unlike the Temples we've encountered thusfar. We will not transit directly to it from the Malkuth Temple; instead we will journey down a path which cuts through Nature's wild outdoors, eventually leading us to the Netzach Temple. As we journey along this path, we will encounter a series of things which will elicit responses from us. Each experience will be an exercise in looking beyond the secondary rational form, and striving to perceive the primary response in its unmodified state. When we reach the Netzach Temple itself, we will strive to experience the even deeper level of the thing itself which incites our primary, gut level response.

The form seldom matches the wholeness of the force. In other words, our rational responses seldom look like our primary emotional reactions, and even less like the things themselves to which we are responding. This can lead to misunderstanding of the thing encountered, an understanding based more upon self's response than upon the thing itself that we're trying to understand. The journey to the Netzach Temple attempts to strip away these layers of rational obfuscation and brings one, step by step, from the rationally modified response; to the deeper, emotional, gut level reaction; and on to the final destination of a non-reactionary perception of the unmodified force itself.

In the realm of Netzach, all roads lead to center, where the Temple is located. The Temple, like all of Netzach, is itself alive and evokes a strong emotional response by virtue of its lush, verdant beauty.

The Temple expresses 7 levels:

1) Ground level -- across which our path leads us, from which all life springs, and to which all life returns. As we journey along this path, we encounter a series of beings. Each one will elicit a response

from us. Our task is to reach deeply into the mechanics of our faculty of perception and let the rational form lead us to a perception of the primary, gut level reaction. Then we follow the gut level till it leads us to a perception of the thing itself, the unmodified force.

2 thru 6) Five steps upward, each a level of clearer understanding. These steps echo the incidents of the journey along the path to the Netzach Temple which strip away the rational obfuscations. The number five implies willfulness -- these steps must be trod with conscious intention. The sixth (solar) level is the ground to which the unmodified life force itself descends.

7) The seventh level is where we encounter the thing itself, stripped of rational modifications. This seventh level is depicted here as a seven-sided font covered by a cupola formed by seven trees, supporting seven stained-glass heptangles, and surmounted by the sign of the planet Venus.

If we have consciously stripped away the rational modifications which obscure our understanding of the root force, we will be granted a clear vision within the font's pool of water. We can then, as Botticelli's famous painting suggests, call Venus forth from the water and experience her meaning directly.

MEDITATION #4: NETZACH

Begin as usual: pass through the Cave Entrance, along the Tunnel passage, up the ten steps, and into the Malkuth Temple where I stand awaiting your arrival.

When all the participants have arrived, I will gather us together and cast a ritual circle.

Once our circle is cast, we will spend several moments together in the center of the Malkuth Temple, holding hands in a circle and bringing our awareness of the presences of the other participants into focus. As you look around the circle, try to sense the unique presence of each participant.

At the appropriate moment, I will bring our focus to the East quarter altar -- our gateway to Netzach. Upon the altar there now sits a beautiful work in stained-glass and behind it we see the same curtain and symbol we encounter at the Cave Entrance.

I light the candles upon the altar, then together, as with a single voice, we speak the phrase: "I-H-V-H Tzabauth (pronounced "yawd-hay-vawv-hay tzaw-baw-ooth"), please guide me to Netzach."

In answer to our prayer, the Hebrew letters יהוה צבאות (IHVH TzBAUTh) appear near the top of the curtain, as if written with light. The upward pointing white triangle shines forth, as does the lowest sphere on the right-hand pillar, and a soft light glows behind the curtain.

When we see this illumination, I reach forward and draw the curtain aside. Hand-in-hand, we all pass through the archway.

We find ourselves standing at the beginning of a path composed of alternating black and white hewn stone. It is a dark night and our only light comes from the stars which fill the sky. The starlight allows us to see that our path cuts through a wild territory, full of dense bramble and oddly shaped, menacing trees.

Together, we begin to walk down the path. Soon we hear the noises of wild animals crashing through the underbrush. It sounds like they are huge and that they are coming up behind us in rapid pursuit.

In fear -- for indeed these creatures are making fearsome grunts, growls, and snarls that communicate to us a clear sense of personal danger -- we try to out run our pursuers.

Oddly, each step we take down this path moves us forward, not only in distance, but also in time. As we run, time passes quickly and the sky begins to brighten with the rising full moon. We seem to have come several miles very quickly, and in the moon's light we see that before us looms an un-climbable wall. Behind us we see our pursuers in the distance -- now in the moonlight, we can tell that there are two of them, still running after us.

The path leads us to a heavy wooden door, the only way through the wall. The wall seems to stretch as far as the eye can see to left and right. We try to open the door but cannot. We pound on it loudly in desperation, for our pursuers come closer and closer with each wasted moment.

Finally, we have no where to go: no where to hide and no way to make it past the wall which blocks our progress. So, we turn to defend ourselves against our pursuers. Just as we turn, they arrive. Growling, they emerge from the shadows and step into a beam of moonlight.

Ha! In the bright moonlight, we see that they are only a couple of tail-wagging dogs and not the vicious, man-eating creatures we had imagined. Our fear changes to relief as we greet these animals and find them friendly.

Just then the door in the wall opens and a tall, powerfully built man, dressed in skins and holding a staff, emerges. He introduces himself as the guardian of the gate and tells us about his dogs. They are the guardians of the path who carefully herd travelers to the safety of the gate. While herding, they naturally bark and growl to keep the wilder beasts away from their flock of travelers. At no time were we in danger from his dogs, in fact they were there only to assure our safe passage!

The guardian is friendly and guides us through the gate to the other side of the wall. Here the path leads onward through a tamer territory. The guardian of the gate sends his dogs with us as travelling companions and guides -- there is no longer a need for them to protect us now that we are on this side of the wall. The full moon is now very high in the sky and we have plenty of silvery light to see our way.

With renewed vigor and joy, we continue down the path. Time and distance pass quickly with each step. We cross over a hill and descend into a great valley. The views are breathtaking in the moonlight!

Just as the moon is setting behind us and the sun dawning ahead of us, the path leads us to the banks of a river. The color of the dawn reflects golden upon the river's surface. We cannot see into the water to gauge the depth of its crossing, but cross it we must since the path disappears at the water's edge and reappears on the opposite bank.

To our left a few paces we notice someone in a dark overcoat, crouched at the water's edge, crying. He wails that he is afraid to cross so wide and deep a river for fear of drowning. Yet he mumbles about his longing to cross, about his longing for the goal of journey's end, which calls to him and causes him anguish. He confronts his fear but does not penetrate it, and now he crouches weeping in frustration and powerlessness, torn between two pressing needs: the safety of self-preservation and the risk of self-growth.

To our right, we see another person, this one is bathing herself at the water's edge. She squats naked, close to the river's ear, and sings a prayer. She asks the river to cleanse her of her fear and to please, please bless her crossing. At this, she dives into the river and swims toward the opposite shore. It is a difficult swim but she is strong and determined. She is blessed by the river and emerges safely to continue her journey. Perhaps we will see her again later.

As the sun peeks over the hills opposite and its first rays enter the valley, our dog guides give a bark and lead us right into the water at the end of the path. They splash along playfully and without fear. To our surprise, the water is only up to their knees and gets no deeper the farther out they go. A ray of sunlight reveals that the path is just under the surface of the water and leads straight across with safety!

Realizing that there is no need for fear, we communicate this to the weeping fellow. He arises and accompanies us across the river. As we cross, we bathe ourselves in the water and sing our own prayers of thanksgiving. The whole body of the sun crests over the hilltops just as we step onto the opposite shore.

In the sun's fullness, the formerly weeping fellow reveals his true self. His dark overcoat unfolds as pure white wings and there before us stands our radiant friend, Raphael. S/He, the Guardian of the East and the element Air, is guardian of the Water's crossing. As the weeping fellow, he showed us a respect for caution; as the naked swimmer, she showed us respect for faith. Together, they delayed us till the sunlight revealed our true path. Here on the opposite shore, in the full sunlight, the two rejoin and reveal themselves to be Raphael. We too have been blessed by the river!

We continue our journey down the black and white stone path. Now we walk in the full light of day and can see the Netzach Temple, though it's still a fair ways off. Not far to left and right, we can see other paths converging upon the Temple. Here and there, we can see other beings. Some are walking determinedly along a path; others seem to be wandering aimlessly between the paths; and still others seem to be engaged in focused activity, as if enacting some sort of personal drama. Everywhere around us we see life and more than just seeing it, we feel it.

At last we arrive at the Temple. The sun has progressed past its zenith and now slants into the Temple from the west.

As you climb the five steps upward, review the lessons we learned from the incidents of our journey along the path.

We gather to hold hands in a circle around the central seven-sided font and I call out the name "IHVH Tzabauth". We look into the font and there see Venus emerging from the water. She wears our own faces, and yet she wears all faces at once. Venus stands in the font and we bask reverently in the love she showers upon us.

We each have our private words with her . . .

At the appropriate moment, I will gather our focus together and we will thank Venus for her graciousness. Then together, as with one voice, we speak the word "Malkuth", which transits us gently back to the center of the Malkuth Temple.

After a few moments of re-orientation, I will release the circle casting. Participants will then exit as usual: down the stairs, along the tunnel, and out the Cave entrance, ultimately returning to normal physical awareness.

63

Follow-up Work

As always, write down some notes summarizing your experience.

In the days immediately following your Netzach meditation, pay close attention to the incidents of your life. Try to see through their surface appearance to their underlying meaning.

Return regularly to the Netzach Temple and seek counsel regarding the meaning of specific events in your life and of specific aspects of your personality. As you follow the path from the Malkuth Temple, allow yourself to encounter whatever your journey presents. Invariably, Netzach will speak to you through symbols in a manner similar to -- though more spontaneous than -- this scripted meditation.

The Netzach Temple is an asset similar to the Hod Temple. Here you can increase your emotional understanding of things. Use this asset, just like you used Hod's rationality, to supplement your work of self-crafting your personality. Pursue conversations with each of the relevant emotional archetypes available in Netzach and thoroughly explore this realm.

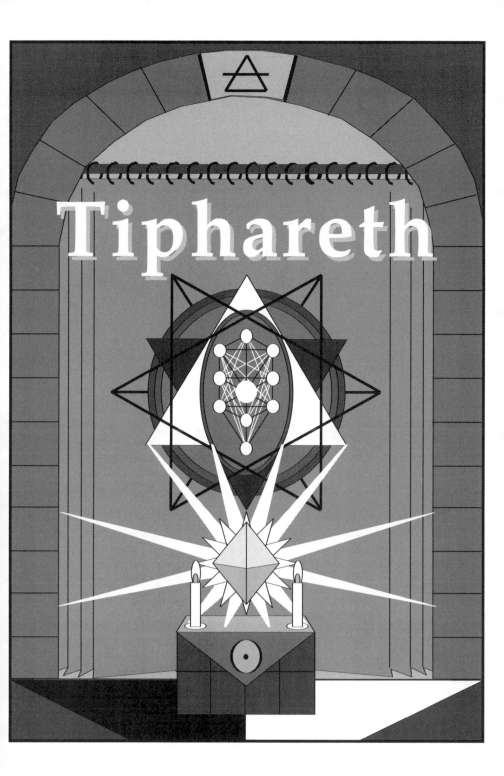

Introduction

The Hebrew word Tiphareth (pronounced "tiff-uh-reth") is generally translated into English as "beauty". As a hieroglyphic construct, the Hebrew word Tiphareth (תפארת) depicts a radiant, expressive thing, adorned on all sides with splendorous garments. Implied here is an image of the Sun, clothed below by the inner planets of the personal-self (Earth, Moon, Mercury and Venus), and clothed above by the outer planets of the more universal self (Mars, Jupiter and Saturn). The image of the Sun, thus adorned, is indeed one of precious beauty!

The Sun represents balance, but this balance is not a static thing. Here, it is that very dynamic state called equilibrium, the achieving of which requires constant equilibration and micro-management. Equilibration is the weaving together of many opposing forces, an act which requires a constancy of attention.

The Solar-self, or Individual-self, is the part of us that has this constancy of attention. It is the Individual-self who incarnates, manifesting the personalities and physical bodies necessary to material life. Over and over, throughout eons of time, the essentially mental Individual-self projects itself downward into the astral and physical levels, shining through each incarnated personality as the link of consistency tying them all together. Through successive incarnations, it learns and evolves, and eventually it fully self-realizes.

Tiphareth brings us back to the Middle Pillar of the Tree of Life. This Middle Pillar defines the rudimentary levels of self-awareness. At the bottom lies Malkuth (sphere #10), representing our physical consciousness of self. Yesod (#9) follows and represents our astral personality, the components of which are defined by Hod (#8) and Netzach (#7). Above the personality, lies the Individual-self represented by Tiphareth (#6). The components of the Individuality likewise, are

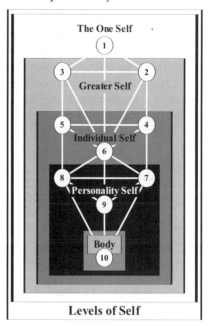

Levels of Self

defined by the higher planets Mars (#5) and Jupiter (#4).

In the course of its existence, an Individual-self will manifest many different, personalities and physical bodies, each limited to a few decades duration. The Tree of Life diagram however, illustrates what the connections between an Individual and only one of its incarnations looks like. It does not depict the fact that an Individual is orbited by many, many such manifestations of itself. It is this multitude of incarnations which forms the lower garment alluded to in the hieroglyphic meaning of the word Tiphareth.

The upper garment of the Individual-self is the universal influx of light in which we all partake. This is symbolized by the spheres numbered 1, 2 and 3. Only the lowest of which is given a planetary attribution (Saturn, #3). By this we are to understand that only a small portion of this higher influx can be symbolized -- the rest remains forever incommunicable, forever incapable of symbolization. In other words, the realm of Unitary consciousness hinted at by the uppermost spheres, can only be understood by direct experience.

As the Tree of Life illustrates, the Individual-self is the level at which we contact that higher influx directly. If we seek it directly from the physical level, we look up and find that intermediary levels of self stand between it and ourselves. Likewise, that higher influx must pass downward through these same intermediary levels of expression before it reaches the physical level.

The practical consequence here is that our consciousness must rise from physical-self, to personal-self, and from there on up to Individual-self, if we wish to experience the higher influx directly.

This fact of nature is used to advantage in a path of initiation (any course of intentional self-realization). The initiate takes responsibility for the personality and consciously self-crafts a personality and life circumstance that more clearly reflects the Individual level of self. In this way, the flow of light from Individual to personal levels of self occurs with less mediation.

When that same process is carried out upon the Individual-self and the Individual consciously self-crafts an Individuality that more clearly expresses the influx of higher light, then the flow of light between the Greater and the Individual levels of self also occurs with less mediation. The end result is that the connection between the higher influx and the physical manifestation becomes so clear as to be functionally a direct connection.

Tiphareth has two basic faces. The first is its inward and upward looking receipt of the higher light. The second face is its downward and outward looking radiation of that light into personal and physical manifestation. Our Tiphareth meditation will touch upon both these aspects.

To reach Tiphareth, we will first pass from Malkuth to our familiar Yesod Temple, rising from physicality to personality. Then from Yesod, we will rise to Tiphareth. This is called "rising on the planes" and is a form of sphere-working which has very integrating effects upon the internal structure of the self.

Once we reach Tiphareth, we will explore the Individual perspective. At first, the experience is one of looking down upon one's personality and physical life circumstance with a surprising degree of detachment. From Tiphareth, the petty concerns of daily life are seen from a much broader perspective and one's relationship with the universe is fixed in a more inclusive context than the merely personal.

After examining our current radiation, we will then turn our attention upward and examine the influx of higher light.

The Tiphareth Temple exists at the very center of a large city. This city is none other than the fabled City of Gold, where the buildings are all built from bricks of solid gold and the streets are cobbled with more of the same. Everything is decorated with the most precious jewels, but most especially, with perfect diamonds. In full sunlight -- and the City of Gold always stands in the full sunlight -- it is a nearly blinding sight.

The City has 12 sides (though some say it has 16), each of which corresponds to one of the 12 signs of the zodiac. This 12-ness is reflected throughout all the City's structures, including the central Temple.

The Temple itself is the City's innermost chamber, its Holy of Holies. It is the point of equilibrium and the place where equilibration is enacted. At the center of the Temple, there floats an immense, radiant diamond, suspended in mid air over a six-sided pool of absorbent blackness.

The diamond has 400 perfectly cut facets, each of which radiates a clear brilliance far brighter than a hundred suns.

The six-sided pool is actually an opening in the floor through which the diamond radiates its light into the relative blackness of astral and material substance. Through this hole, we will look down to our current personas (Yesod) and life circumstances (Malkuth).

The broadsword that lies upon the edge of the pool, represents the power that the Individual-self wields over the personal and physical aspects of self. It is also a complex statement about the nature of time, referring to the only place where power is truly wielded -- the now.

At the personal, physical level, we experience now only from a present-moment perspective. Our present-moment is of immeasurably brief duration and seems to move ever forward. It's that cutting-edge where what-has-been meets the ever-new face of what-will-be. The present-moment is thus a dynamic state of constant change -- it is the only place where we can wield our power to self-craft.

The Individual however, has a broader experience of now, one whose present-moment includes the whole portion of eternity that has thusfar transpired for it. The Individual therefore wields power within a now that includes all of its "past" incarnations. Its experience of now is of the same quality as our personal experience, except that the Individual's now is inclusive of a larger quantity of time. For the Individual, what-has-been and what-is are intimately united in the experience of the present-moment.

Thus the broadsword represents: #1) the Individual's power to project its will (its light) down into the specificity of time-space and personal incarnation; and #2) the Personality's power within its present-moment now, to wield that higher light and self-craft.

Each of the 12 walls of the Temple are marked with one of the signs of the zodiac. Below each, there is a curtained archway, through which flashes the same sign. This is meant to symbolize the two aspects of these archways.

Their first aspect is that they lead outward into the City of Gold, each offering a different tour of the City. Since the City symbolizes the Individual's entire body of incarnations, exploration of it opens the initiate to past memories and their attendant responsibilities.

Their second aspect, the aspect we'll be exploring in our meditation, is that they are also doorways that let in the 12 zodiacal influences. The influx of these 12 universal influences combine to form the white brilliance radiated by the central diamond.

There is no ceiling to the Tiphareth Temple. Instead, it opens onto the star-filled depths of outer space. This is a paradox, considering that if you pass through one of the archways and step out into the City of Gold, the sky above is filled by the light of a single sun.

This day-star symbolizes the constancy of the Individual's influence throughout the body of its incarnations. The stars seen in the sky from within the Temple however, symbolize the Individual's context within the greater universe. Each of those stars strewn across the infinite depths of outer space, is a similar City of Gold -- each one of which is equilibrated by a unique Individual-self.

MEDITATION #5: TIPHARETH

Begin as usual: pass through the Cave Entrance, along the Tunnel passage, up the ten steps, and into the Malkuth Temple where I stand awaiting your arrival.

When all the participants have arrived, I will gather us together and cast a ritual circle.

Once our circle is cast, we will spend several moments together in the center of the Malkuth Temple, holding hands in a circle and bringing our awareness of the presences of the other participants into focus. As you look around the circle, try to sense the unique presence of each participant.

At the appropriate moment, I will bring our focus to the East quarter altar -- our gateway to Tiphareth. Hovering over the altar, we see a large cut diamond which seems to shine with an inner light. Behind this we see the same curtain and symbol we encounter at the Cave Entrance.

I light the candles upon the altar, then we speak the phrase: "IHVH A-donai (pronounced "yawd-hay-vawv-hay ah-doh-nye"), please guide me to Tiphareth."

In answer to our prayer, the Hebrew letters יהוה אדני (IHVH ADNI) appear near the top of the curtain, as if written with light.

The upward pointing white triangle shines forth, as does the center-most sphere on the middle pillar, and a soft light glows behind the curtain.

When we see this illumination, I reach forward and draw the curtain aside. Hand-in-hand, we all pass through the archway.

There is a roll of distant thunder and we find ourselves standing at the center of the familiar Yesod Temple. We rejoin into a circle and orient ourselves.

At this point, please take a few moments to sense your separation from your physical body, and consciously align yourself with your personality-self. Once again, briefly note the nine faces mirrored back at you, but don't tarry there.

At the appropriate moment, I will direct our attention upwards to the ceiling of the Yesod Temple. At its center, we see a six-sided opening and through it streams a ray of sunlight.

I call out the Name "IHVH Adonai" several times and this ray of light first brightens, and then descends to engulf our circle. It grabs hold of us, as if we've been pulled to heel by an irresistible magnet, and then it whisks us upward through the hole in the ceiling. At the speed of light, we are transported to the center of the Tiphareth Temple . . .

Everywhere there are gold surfaces, flashing with the glint of diamond-light. The Temple it seems, is composed solely of light, molded into form by the force of the central diamond's gravity.

73

We take a few moments to orient ourselves and then we turn our attention to the six-sided pool. We each kneel down at a separate side and gaze into the pool's inky blackness. Look deep into the pool and with your mind, follow the ray of diamond-light down to Yesod, seeing there your personality-self. Sense your separation from it.

Now follow that ray of light as it reaches further down to touch Malkuth. See your physical body and your particular life circumstance, illumined below in Malkuth, and sense your separation from them. Concentrate closely on this feeling of detachment from your personal and physical selves.

When you succeed in achieving this detached perspective and are relatively comfortable with it, turn your attention to your connection with your personal and physical selves. In your mind, again follow that ray of diamond-light downwards, but this time instead of focusing upon your separation from the bodies it illumines, focus upon the light's ability to connect these parts of yourself. Feel now how your Tiphareth, Yesod and Malkuth are joined together by force of light and gravity.

Once you've experienced the light's downward permeation and connection of your Individual, Personal and physical selves, turn your attention upward and follow the diamond-light back to a detached perspective.

At the appropriate moment, when all have once again achieved detachment from their personal and physical selves, I will gather our attention upon the radiant Diamond, hovering over the pool. We will then spend several minutes in private meditation upon this Diamond.

I suggest you focus first upon the Diamond's radiation of light. Bask in its glow and feel how it's light permeates you through and through.

Second, focus upon becoming this light. Feel yourself composed of this light, molded to your unique form by force of gravity. Let the whole substance of your body be this light.

Third, focus upon merging your light-body self with the radiant Diamond. Your light-body passes easily into the Diamond and you look outwards from inside of it.

Finally, focus upon radiating the light of your conjoined light-body/Diamond self. As you stand within the Diamond, looking out, consciously radiate your unique, Individual Diamond-light. Gaze below you and willfully permeate your personal and physical selves, through and through, with your Diamond-light.

At the appropriate moment, I will call you each back from your meditations and we will again join hands in a circle. I will then lead us in a brief tour of the 12 archways.

At each archway, I speak the Name "IHVH Adonai". This causes the zodiacal sign to appear, written in light upon the curtain. As I pull aside the curtain, the influence of that sign enters the Temple, providing us the opportunity to sense its particularities of flavor. In this way, we will gain a brief taste-sample of all 12 zodiacal influences -- these are the universal influences equilibrated by the Individual, Diamond-self, who essentially transforms influences into radiant light.

We will end our time in the Tiphareth Temple, holding hands in a circle, basking in the Diamond's light, and joined together in a prayer of thanksgiving. Our thankfulness is for this blessing of light which permeates each of our lives, through and through.

Together, as with a single voice, we speak the word "Malkuth". With a gentle sense of falling, we descend through the floor, pass down through the Yesod Temple, and are deposited softly upon the floor of the Malkuth Temple. The transit's feeling is one of gravity-powered descent, of re-integration and of re-attachment.

After a few moments of re-orientation, I will release the circle casting. Participants will then exit as usual: down the stairs, along the tunnel, and out the Cave entrance, ultimately returning to normal physical awareness.

Follow-up Work

As always, write down some notes summarizing your experience.

Return regularly to the Tiphareth Temple and examine both the personality you manifest and the life circumstance you enact. Look with an eye to see in what ways these reflect the Diamond-light of your Individual-self. In what ways can you more clearly express that inner light?

Apply what you learn to the process of self-crafting your personality. Strive to express the Diamond-light of your Individual-self with clarity and self-craft a personality that is a direct manifestation of that light.

When you have met with significant success in your efforts, broaden your perspective and begin exploring the 12 zodiacal archways. First explore the zodiacal influences which enter the Temple through them and then, pass through the archways and explore the City of Gold.

Always apply what you learn to your efforts at self-crafting. Constantly refine yourself.

Spend some time in Tiphareth meditating upon the subject of time. Focus upon your experience of time: upon how we naturally sequentialize it into past-present-future, and upon the essential now-ness of the present-moment. Examine the nature of your connection to the present-moment especially. This meditation upon time will better prepare you for the upcoming Temple meditations.

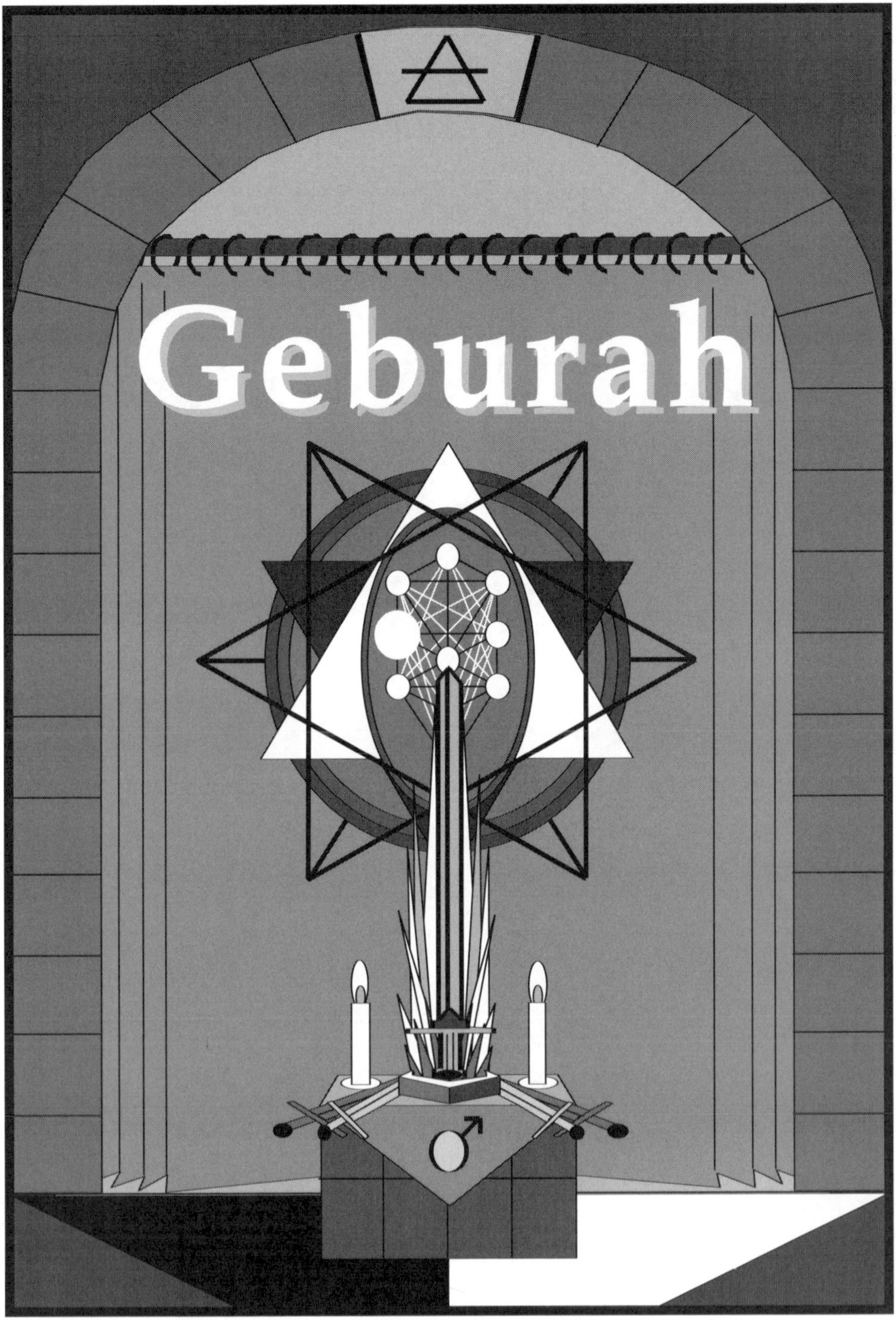
Geburah

Introduction

Similar to our rise above Yesod, which took us to Form/Hod and then to Force/Netzach, our rise above Tiphareth takes us again to the polarized side pillars of Force and Form.   At the level of the Individual-Self, the pole of Form is represented by Geburah (pronounced "gebb-you-ruh") which means "strength, might, power" and corresponds to the red planet Mars. Force is represented by Gedulah (pronounced "gedd-you-lah") meaning "greatness, majesty, magnificence", and corresponds to the planet Jupiter.

Above these, defining their orbits and representing a level of Self still more subtle and vastly more inclusive than the Individual, stands Binah/Saturn. Now even though Binah/Saturn (sphere 3) stands on the side pillar of Form, it represents a non-polarized state of being. This is a level at which all poles are reconciled and where all opposites are united.

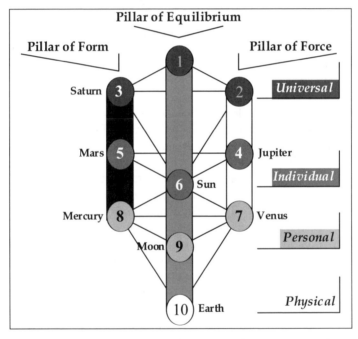

In ancient astrology, Saturn was seen as the outermost planet and thus it came to represent the boundaries of human experience. It's orbit symbolically and factually contained, encompassed, included the orbits and influences of all the inner planets. It represented the interface between the Divine and the human -- that face of Divinity that we humans could actually see (hence it's position here at the top of the pillar of Form).

To understand the significance of Geburah/Mars and the meaning of our Temple, I'll need to first establish a context for it and that will require a little 'round-about explaining. You might have to read what follows a few times for it to make sense ...

Binah (pronounced "bee-nuh", means "understanding, discernment, intelligence") exists outside the realm of sequence (i.e., space-time). The experience of Binah consciousness brings with it an eternal perspective, one from which the whole infinity of time-space-sequence is seen simultaneously. The Binah experience is not broken down into past-present-future or beginning-middle-end, instead it is non-sequential. Beginning, middle and end are experienced/perceived as things which exist simultaneously, instead of as separate things which follow each other. Past, present and future are encompassed within a single now and experienced non-sequentially with the same quality of now-ness that we experience only with the physical present-moment.

Binah/Saturn holds within itself the non-sequentialized potential for all things, but those things are not manifest -- at least not with finality -- at the level of Binah itself. The first stage in the manifestation of Binah's potential is the process of sequentialization, or the placement of things into relationship and order.

This sequentialization of non-sequentialized potential passes through two poles before it attains to an integral balance (Tiphareth). The first pole is inclusiveness, symbolized by Gedulah/Jupiter (sphere 4). Here the factor of similarity is introduced and the potentials are connected by virtue of the natural attraction that 'like' has with 'like'. Sequence at this level/stage, is not based upon differentiation per se, but upon commonality. Thus Gedulah/Jupiter is also given the title Chesed, which means "mercy, compassion, loving kindness".

The second pole is that of exclusiveness, symbolized by Geburah/Mars (sphere 5). Here the factor of difference is introduced and the potentials, which have already been set into relationship based upon their commonalities, are now separated by virtue of their differences. 'Like' is separated from 'unlike' -- 'self' defines 'other'. Sequence at this stage/level, is not based upon attraction, but upon repulsion. Thus we speak of severity, strength (Geburah), and fear (Pachad -- another title for sphere 5).

By the level of Geburah/Mars, the non-sequentialized potentials of Binah/Saturn are fairly well defined as sequential, Individual things. Each separate thing at the level of Geburah, is a manifestation of a limited part of the infinite Binah-potential. Here the perspective/experience of existence is contextual and sequential. There is, at this level, a division of experience into past-present-future, one thought follows another, etc.

In the Western Hermetic Tradition of Qabbala, the Tarot card *VII: The Chariot* expresses the connection between non-sequential Binah/Saturn and sequentialized Geburah/Mars. This Tarot image depicts the commonality which links the Geburian Individual to the Binah-wholeness -- i.e., the now-ness of conscious awareness.

VII: The Chariot

VII: The Chariot depicts the experience that a sequentialized consciousness has of space-time-sequence. The charioteer represents the individual, sequentialized unit of conscious awareness itself. The chariot represents the present-moment -- the only place where we experience now-ness. The smallness of the chariot (present-moment) confines the charioteer and symbolically defines the limits of a sequentialized consciousness's power.

Behind the chariot, back along the road it has followed, we see buildings and hills. These represent the past which has crystallized into a coherent form by its "passage" from present-moments into past-moments.

The chariot faces forward and seems to emerge from the two-dimensional card. This represents the sequentialized individual's relationship with the future. To the present-moment, the future stands as a different dimension.

In fact, the present-moment is an illusion for it is a thing of infinitely minute duration. It is not a thing, in and of itself, but is in reality the knife-edge interface of past and future. The present-moment is where the body-of-the-past (what is), is touched by the ceaseless force of change (what will-be). That touching is continuous and is not itself sequential -- never are past and future separate.

The sequentialized individual's experience of the present-moment has a certain quality of now-ness to it. This quality of now-ness is the same as the now-ness with which the Binah-consciousness experiences past, present and future simultaneously. The difference is that instead of encompassing only the present-moment interface of past and future, Binah's now encompasses past AND present AND future, simultaneously.

VII: The Chariot is telling us that the now-ness of our present-moment is what connects the Individual to Binah. By expanding that now-ness beyond the limits of the sequentialized present-moment, one connects with the non-sequential, all-inclusive perspective of Binah/Saturn.

Geburah/Mars implies action, power, decision and judgment. At this level, the chariot seems to move ever-forward through the sequence of time-space. In different versions of the Tarot image this sense of motive power is expressed in different ways. In some, the wheels spin and the chariot is drawn along the road by creatures, clearly symbolizing the seeming forwardness of the present-moment's movement through time; yet in others, the creatures rest and the wheels are stationary.

This latter speaks to the illusory nature of the "passage" of time. In a sense, the Individual does not pass through time; rather, the individual is stationary and time-space moves around it. The sequentialized consciousness is always riding in the enclosure of the present-moment and it is the sameness and constancy of the now-ness of that experience which defines Individual consciousness.

As incarnate humans, we either "ride" the chariot of the present-moment or we take up the reins and "drive" the chariot. Driving the chariot is a Geburian act involving judgment, severity, decision, etc.

The Geburah Temple symbolizes our power to drive this chariot of present-moment now-ness. The Temple's five-fold structure is based upon the primary symbol of the human power to enact its own

Individual will -- the pentagram.

The pentagram's topmost point is attributed to Aethyr -- the singular Element of commonality. This corresponds to the Binah-potentials which have been sequentialized by their descent through the Force-pole of Gedulah (sphere 4) and arranged according to their Jupiterian commonality. The Aethyr therefore, is the Force which connects all things. In *VII: The Chariot,* the universal Aethyr is represented at the Individual level by the charioteer her/himself.

The pentagram's four lower points are attributed to the familiar Four Elements. These represent the phases of differentiation through which the unifying Aethyr passes as it descends into manifestation. They correspond to the four-sided enclosure of the chariot itself in *VII: The Chariot,* implying that the Aethyr has power only within the confines of the present-moment's now-ness.

Another way of putting it is to say that the Aethyr manifests (an act of differentiation) its potentials through the Four Elements. This dynamic passage into differentiation is what the pentagram symbolizes. Following the figure's lines, Aethyr descends into Fire, passes to Air, then Water and finally Earth, at which point it then returns to Aethyr. This endless, sequential cycling of the Aethyr through the Four Elements and back to Aethyr, is called the "rotation of the Elements".

The pentagram is used in modern ritual to effect either the descent of the Aethyr/will-Force into manifest Elemental-Form, or conversely, to effect the Aethyr's ascent from Form

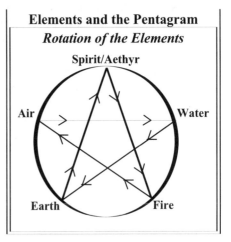

Elements and the Pentagram

Rotation of the Elements

Spirit/Aethyr

Air / Water

Earth / Fire

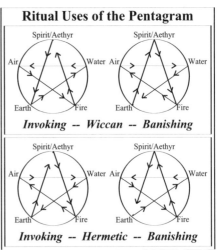

Ritual Uses of the Pentagram

Invoking -- Wiccan -- Banishing

Invoking -- Hermetic -- Banishing

83

back to Force. In practical terms, the pentagram is employed to "invoke" or to "banish" a specific Force.

There are several opinions about what constitutes an invoking and a banishing pentagram. In the Wiccan tradition that I learned, a witch invokes the Spirit by bringing the Aethyr down to Earth, then up to Water, over to Air, down to Fire and back up to Aethyr. Banishing takes an opposite direction and starts from Earth, banishes toward Aethyr, descends to Fire, rises to Air, over to Water, and ends in Earth.

The Hermetic tradition I learned employs the pentagram differently, following more closely the "rotation of the Elements" and a clockwise=invoking, counter-clockwise=banishing approach.

These differences in the pentagram's usage illustrate the differences in basic philosophy between these two Traditions. Each way represents a slightly different approach to the use of power/Force. The Hermetic way is very rational, scientific and follows an archetypal mental pattern, while the Wiccan way is very gut-level, intuitive and earthy, following a very practical experiential pattern. To my mind, the Hermetic way accords with the overtly masculine image of the Roman god of war, Mars. The Wiccan way on the other hand, accords with a broader, more inclusive feminist image of powerfulness.

For example, a witch invokes by drawing the Aethyr directly into the physical vessel (Earth). Once planted (earthed), it rises/evolves/matures upwards through the Elements, eventually reaching Aethyr again. Its passage through the Elements changes it -- its return to Aethyr is thus a process of self-realization. Likewise, a witch banishes directly from Earth toward Aethyr -- immediately releasing the Force from its Form -- and then follows it back down into the Earth. Its passage downward through the Elemental sequence changes it, so it returns to Earth purified and assumes a more self-realized Form. For the witch, both the invoking and the banishing are blessings which empower a process of self-realization and growth.

The pentagram of the Hermetic is more goal oriented than process oriented. The Hermetic magician invokes by drawing the Aethyr/Force down into Earth/Form through the descending Elemental sequence. This process is one of differentiation and of accruing material form to a core inspiration. Once it reaches the density of Elemental Earth, the return/ascent to Aethyr merely reconnects the Form with its internal Force. This establishes a closed, Individualized form -- the goal, as it were.

The Hermetic likewise banishes with a goal-orientation. The banishing starts with Earth/Form and proceeds up the scale of Elements till it reaches a rarified, purified Aethyr state. Once cleansed in this way, the Aethyr/Force is brought back down directly into an Earth/Form of the magician's choosing. Again, it establishes a closed, Individualized form/goal.

The Geburah Temple is designed to accommodate either manner of working and we will be exploring both approaches in our meditation.

At each of the Temple's five sides, there stands an archway, across which hangs a curtain embroidered with a corresponding Elemental symbol. These symbols are the standard "Tools of the Elements" used by the magician. Each one represents how we use the Elements to enact/realize our Individual will.

Magical Tools

Aethyr Wheel   Fire Wand   Air Knife   Water Chalice   Earth Pentacle

Mars Sword

The Aethyr Wheel has five parts: one center for Aethyr; three lines intersecting center for the Elements Fire, Air and Water (they radiate from center, polarized into three positive and three negative poles); and one circumference for the Element Earth. Thus it symbolizes the potential for differentiation. It is a wheel specifically because it is a dynamic thing which we can set into motion.

Following the rotation of the Elements sequence, the motive Aethyr is directed through the Fire Wand, giving it a specific, unified direction and orienting it toward a specific goal with all one's force of will. The Fire is directed through the Air Knife and differentiated by virtue of what it is and is not to be, with all one's force of intellect. The differentiated Air is directed through the Water Chalice and is personalized with all the passion of one's desire for this thing. The per-sonalized Water is directed through the Earth Pentacle where all the forces are bound together naturally into specific material form.

These tools also function in the opposite sequence: The Earth/Form is unbound from the Pentacle and reduced to a Chalice-held liquid. The Water is poured from the Chalice and the vapor of it is gathered up by the Air Knife. The Knife disperses the Air, reducing it to pure energy. The energy is drawn into the Fire Wand and emerges as pure light. The light is drawn into the dark center of the spinning Aethyr Wheel, etc.

The Elemental tools are wielded within the context of a ritual Circle. The magical "casting" of that Circle is performed with the Mars Sword. This is the same broadsword we saw resting upon the edge of the pool in our Tiphareth Temple.

As before, the Sword represents two things: One, it represents the Individual's ability to wield power over the personal and physical aspects of self. In this sense, the Sword symbolizes several different approaches to the use of that power -- a sword can be used to defend, to attack, to incise, sever, divide, destroy, preserve, define, or even to slice the ritual bread for feast. However it is used, due to its size and weight, the Mars Sword takes two hands to wield. In other words, it takes the whole of the Individual -- both poles of Mercy/Force and Severity/Form -- to wield the Sword. Since it requires balance to hold a broadsword and to flail it about without toppling yourself over in the process, only the Individual-self, rooted in the Tiphareth equilibri-um, can wield the Mars Sword effectively. This aspect of the Sword also implies great responsibility, for it is hard to halt the swing of a broadsword once you've started the motion. The weight of the thing moves with its own momentum once you've set it into motion, so great care must be taken in its wielding.

The second thing the Sword represents, is the now-ness of the Individual's present-moment. The Sword defines the present-moment as the cutting-edge interface of what-has-been (past) and what-will-be (future). The Sword divides between the past and the future with the sharpness of its cutting-edge now-ness, creating a micro-thin dimen-sion of its own. In other words, the Sword has power only within the confines of the present-moment's now-ness. Its function is to bring the Jupiterian commonality or proto-sequentialization, into the highly sequentialized realm of the now-ness of a specific present-moment. This is a process of differentiation, definition, individualization, etc.

To introduce you to its use, we will magically "cast" a ritual Circle within the Geburah Temple, using the Mars Sword. The Sword is held with both hands, and the tip of it, pointing outward from the body, is touched to the center of the Aethyr Wheel emblazoned upon the Temple curtain. The Sword draws out the violet Aethyr-light and fills with its power. The Aethyr is then projected outward from the tip of the Sword and a Circle composed of Aethyr is drawn clockwise around the Temple, beginning and ending at the exact center of the Aethyr Wheel. This casting defines the specific present-moment within which we will wield the Elemental power of our now-ness -- our Circle is our Chariot's four-sided enclosure wherein we take up the reins to drive.

The casting with the Sword is repeated as many times as the situation feels to need. If after one casting, you feel satisfied that the Circle is well defined, then once is enough. But if after a single casting, the Circle seems unfinished or not solid enough, then by all means repeat the casting till it does attain a satisfying completeness. As you work, visualize what comes most naturally and intuitively to you, and feel your way through the casting.

Once our Circle is cast, we will explore the use of our power by pursuing work with the two invoking and the two banishing pentagrams outlined earlier. This is going to be an actual magical working so I want you each to give some serious forethought to what you would like to accomplish. For this meditation, you should choose a specific aspect of yourself that you wish to strengthen and empower.

We will be working with Geburah's positive power of nurturance and self-growth, and focusing it upon each of our Individual concerns. We will draw this power down into manifestation through the four Elemental Tools of our specific present-moment's now-ness.

Prior to the Geburah ritual, spend some time meditating upon what aspect of yourself you would like to seriously advance. This must be an aspect that already exists within you to some degree and not just a separate, ideal thing you would like to become. Find something positive about your present self that you would see strengthened and empowered. Once you've made your selection, spend more time meditating upon it alone. Examine this aspect of yourself from as many angles as possible and get to know it as thoroughly as your available time allows.

As a final note, at the center of the Geburah Temple there is a five-sided font of fire. This symbolizes the raw power of Jupiterian-commonality which fills the differentiated now-ness of the specific present-moment. This fire does not burn and consume -- rather, here at the level of Geburah, it warms and nurtures. It is more akin to the dynamic center of the Aethyr Wheel, than to Elemental Fire.

We will be rising along this Geburian Aethyr-fire in our passage from Malkuth to the Geburah Temple. At the end of our ritual, we will follow a different route back to the Malkuth Temple.

MEDITATION #6: GEBURAH

Begin as usual: pass through the Cave Entrance, along the Tunnel passage, up the ten steps, and into the Malkuth Temple where I stand awaiting your arrival.

When all the participants have arrived, I will gather us together and cast a ritual circle.

Once our circle is cast, we will spend several moments together in the center of the Malkuth Temple, holding hands in a circle and bringing our awareness of the presences of the other participants into focus. As you look around the circle, try to sense the unique presence of each participant.

At the appropriate moment, I will bring our focus to the East quarter altar -- our gateway to Geburah. Upon the altar, we see a five-sided font of fire (the Aethyr-fire).

Standing within this fire is the Mars Sword from the Tiphareth Temple (this is my personal Sword). Laid about upon the altar are four more swords. These four are "blanks" -- unempowered, roughly finished swords, that have not yet been tuned to the vibration of a specific Individual.

These are my gifts to each one of you. There is a sword for you and, by symbolic extension, one for each participant who joins us from future moments.

Behind the altar, we see the same curtain and symbol we encounter at the Cave Entrance.

As I light the candles upon the altar, we each grab hold of a sword. Then together, we point our swords toward the Gateway symbol, and with a single voice, we speak the phrase: "Elohim Gibor (pronounced "eh-low-heem gib-boar"), please guide me to Geburah."

In answer to our prayer, the Hebrew letters גבור אלהים (ALHIM GBVR) appear near the top of the curtain, as if written with light. The upward pointing white triangle shines forth, as does the middle sphere on the left-hand pillar, and a soft light glows behind the curtain.

When we see this illumination, I reach forward and draw the curtain aside.

This reveals a realm of purest Aethyr-fire. The force of the Aethyr-fire reaches out gently and, without exceeding our personal limits of comfort, gathers hold of the blade-end of our outstretched swords, drawing us through the archway and then upward. As you are drawn, sword-first, upward through the Aethyr-fire, examine the sword you hold.

Before your eyes, your sword will be refined by its passage through the Aethyr-fire. The dull unfinished blade becomes a sharp and shining thing; the drab handle becomes jewel encrusted; the unadorned blade becomes etched with words and signs which identify it specifically and intimately as your own. This tunes your sword to you Individually and henceforth it can be grasped by no one other than yourself. As you use your Sword, it will continue to evolve and will constantly reflect each one of your actions -- I pray that you create through "right action" a Powerful Sword of Beauty and Loving Kindness.

Our passage through the Aethyr-fire ends with our arrival at the Geburah Temple. We stand before the Aethyr Wheel and take a moment to orient ourselves . . .

Our first task will be to cast the Circle with our Swords. As you raise your Sword and touch its tip to the center of the Aethyr Wheel, focus your mind upon that aspect of yourself you have chosen to empower. As you take the Aethyr into your Sword and then cast the Circle with it, tune your Circle to your chosen concern. In this way,

91

the whole of the Geburah Temple is charged with a focus upon your individual concern.

The Circle is always cast with a clockwise/deosil movement. The natural flow of energy within the Circle is clockwise/deosil, so counter-clockwise movement around a cast Circle, tends to unbind and defeat its power. Counter-clockwise movement is therefore reserved for acts of "banishing" and for "releasing" the cast Circle.

Together, we will cast the Circle three times with a pause after each casting. During each pause we'll examine the effectiveness of our casting. After the third casting, we will set our Swords down upon the edge of the central font of Aethyr-fire. There they will remain till we are through with our work and ready to release our Circle's casting.

Moving clockwise around the Temple, we gather before the Earth Pentacle and focus again upon the aspect of ourselves we wish to strengthen. As you contemplate, cup your hands together in front of you and visualize a smaller Pentacle materializing within them. The Pentacle is inscribed upon a thick disk of solid lead and it fills your hands comfortably. With your mind, make it intimately reflect (through whatever symbols come naturally to you) the *present* state of that aspect of yourself you've chosen to empower. Feel it and see it as a clear representation of how this aspect *currently* manifests in your day-to-day life.

Our next task will be the purification and clarification of our Pentacle. For this we will employ the witch's banishing-pentagram sequence.

This is a two-fold act corresponding to the witches phrase "I cast out all negativity and in its place, let harmony be." We cast out all the negativity residing within our Pentacle by walking with it from the Earth Pentacle archway, across the Temple, to the Aethyr Wheel archway.

We then unbind our Pentacle's form by releasing it into the Aethyr

#1: Witch's Banishing

Spirit/Aethyr

Air

Water

Earth

Fire

Wheel. The circumference of the Wheel draws the Pentacle from our hands and absorbs it. We see our Pentacle's form broken down by the Wheel's internal workings and watch as it's reduced to a force which gravitates to the exact center of the Aethyr Wheel. This "casts out" all the negativity associated with the form that this aspect of yourself currently manifests.

We "let harmony be" by drawing this Aethyr-force from the Wheel's center and then guiding it through the Elements, back down into our Earth Pentacle form. Cup your hands together in front of you and draw your Pentacle's Aethyr-force out from the Wheel's center, letting it fill your hands. Feel and see its fieriness -- this is the living fire which warms and nurtures without burning or consuming.

Pass across the Temple with your handful of Aethyr-fire and stand before the Fire Wand archway. Release your Aethyr-fire into the lower end of the Fire Wand. Now reach up and grasp hold of your own Fire Wand from the curtain. Feel and see it in your hand. Visualize it as being decorated with symbols that clearly represent the aspect of yourself you are concerned with. Fill your Wand with all the intensity of purpose you feel regarding this aspect of yourself. Let the Elemental Fire burn away from the Aethyr-fire, all that is extraneous to this one focus.

Pass across the Temple with your Fire Wand and stand before the Air Knife archway. Touch the upper tip of your Wand to the Air Knife and cause the Fire to pass from Wand into Knife. As a consequence, the Wand in your hand transforms into your Air Knife. Again, feel it and see it. Your Knife is lightweight, razor sharp and fits perfectly in your hand. Fill your Knife with all your thoughts which define this aspect of yourself. With your Knife's sharp blade, trim away from the Fire, all that is extraneous to this one focus. Let your Knife be covered with symbols that intimately and clearly depict this aspect of yourself.

Pass across the Temple with your Air Knife and stand before the Water Chalice archway. Plunge your Knife blade into the cupped Water and pass the Aethyr-Fire-Air power from Knife to Cup. As before, the Knife in your hand transforms into your Water Chalice. Feel it and see it. Your Chalice is finely crafted from the purest silver and decorated with symbols that correspond intimately with this aspect of yourself. Fill your Chalice with all the emotions that bind together your thoughts concerning this aspect of yourself. With your Chalice's Water, wash away from the Air, all that is extraneous and distill from it a singular focus.

Pass across the Temple with your Water Chalice and stand before the Earth Pentacle archway. Hold your Chalice aloft and cast its Aethyr-Fire-Air-Water upon the Earth Pentacle. Within your hands, the emptied Chalice transforms into your heavy, solid Earth Pentacle. Feel and see how your Pentacle has been changed, brightened and clarified by this passage around the witch's banishing pentagram. Its form now more clearly expresses its internal force.

Now that we have banished negativity and established harmony, we will turn to the invocation of greater power into our Pentacle. For this task we will employ the hermetic's invoking-pentagram sequence and draw power into our Pentacle from the Aethyr and then from each of the four Elements.

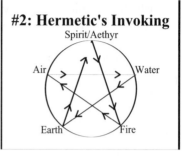

#2: Hermetic's Invoking

Holding your Earth Pentacle before you, pass clockwise around the Temple, past the Air archway, and stand before the Aethyr Wheel. With your mind, draw down a stream of raw Aethyr-fire from the center of the Wheel and cause it to permeate your Pentacle. Feel and see this addition of Aethyr-fire. See how it moves about the lines of your Pentacle, following the Hermetic's invoking sequence 'round and 'round till it is fully integrated into your Pentacle's form.

Pass across the Temple with your Pentacle in hand and stand before the Fire Wand archway. Draw down a stream of raw Fire from the upper end of the Wand and cause it to permeate your Pentacle. Feel and see it circulate around your Pentacle's lines of power, energizing and strengthening all that is Fiery within this aspect of yourself.

Pass across the Temple and repeat this procedure with the Air Knife. Then cross to the Water Chalice, and then to the Earth Pentacle. After you have filled your Pentacle with raw Earth and have seen it circulate and empower all that is Earthy within this aspect of yourself, pass with it again to the Aethyr-Wheel. Hold your greatly empowered Pentacle high over your head and present it as an offering to the Divine.

Our next task is to bless and mature the raw power we have drawn into our Pentacle. For this we will employ the witch's invoking-pentagram sequence.

Raise your empowered Pentacle again to the Aethyr Wheel and ask the Divine to bless it. Feel and see this blessing permeate your Pentacle through and through. The raw Aethyr-fire within it conforms to the highest possible manifestation of this aspect of yourself.

Pass across the Temple to the

#3: Witch's Invoking

Earth Pentacle archway and, holding your Pentacle aloft, ask Gabriel (Guardian of the Element Earth) to bless it. Feel and see this blessing permeate all that is Earthy within this aspect of yourself.

Pass across to the Water Chalice and ask Haniel for her blessing; then across to the Air Knife and Raphael; then across to the Fire Wand and Mikael; and then cross to stand once again before the Aethyr Wheel. Take a few moments to study your Pentacle. Feel and see how it has matured, how all its raw power has been lovingly tamed and directed toward a singular focus -- upon the highest possible manifestation of this aspect of yourself. Your Pentacle is a thing of beauty and power, so offer it up once again as your gift to the Divine.

Our final task is to release from our Pentacle, the power that we have so artfully bound to its specific focus and specific form. For this we will employ the hermetic's banishing-pentagram sequence. With the banishing, we will cast this focused power out of the Pentacle and into manifestation within our Individual lives.

#4: Hermetic's Banishing

With your Pentacle in hand, walk clockwise around the Temple, past the Water and Fire archways and stand before the Earth Pentacle archway. Face the curtain and kneel down. Take a brief moment to fully see your Pentacle's perfection of form and then swiftly smash this beautiful creation onto the stone floor. As you do this, release the beauty and perfection from the Pentacle's form. Simultaneously cast all its focused Earthiness through the archway, into manifestation within your daily life.

The Pentacle rubble in your hands transforms into your beautiful Water Chalice. Carry your Chalice across the Temple to the Water Chalice archway and there pour out its contents upon the stone floor. Release the beauty and perfection from the Chalice's form. Simultaneously cast all its focused Wateriness through the archway, into manifestation within your daily life.

The empty Chalice in your hands transforms into your gleaming Air Knife. Carry your Knife across to the Air Knife archway and in one swift motion, plunge it into the stone floor up to its hilt. Release the beauty and perfection from the Knife's form. Simultaneously cast all its focused Airiness through the archway, into manifestation.

The Knife hilt in your hands transforms into your radiant Fire

Wand. Carry your Wand across to the Fire Wand archway and project all of its power through the archway. Release the beauty and perfection from the Wand's form and cast all its focused Fieriness into manifestation.

The spent, empty Wand in your hands transforms into a small, spinningly alive, Aethyr Wheel. Carry your Wheel across to the Aethyr Wheel archway and offer it up to the Divine. Feel the resonance between your small hand-held Wheel and the greater universal Wheel. Your Wheel is a specific, focused manifestation of that greater Wheel.

Turn now, with your Wheel in hand, toward the Earth Pentacle archway. In one fluid movement, pass across the Temple to the Earth archway and cast your Aethyr Wheel through the archway with all your might. Feel and see it spinning into manifestation throughout the Individual, Personal and Physical levels of your life. It gathers the fibers of your life together and weaves them into its destined focus.

Now turn your back on the Earth Pentacle archway and return, moving clockwise, to the Aethyr Wheel archway. Together, we will say a prayer of thanksgiving to the Divine.

At the appropriate moment, I will direct us to pick up our Swords from the edge of Aethyr-fire font. We will then "release" our Circle casting. We begin by touching our Sword's tip to the center of the Aethyr Wheel. Then, with our Swords extended, we pass counter-clockwise around the Temple and draw the Aethyr-fire of our Circle back into our Swords. We start from the point where we ended our casting, and pass counter-clockwise till we return to the center of the Aethyr Wheel. Thus our releasing's ending point is symbolically the same point as our casting's beginning. Now project the Aethyr-fire you've drawn up from the Circle, out the tip of your Sword and into the exact center of the Aethyr Wheel (from whence it originally came).

Our Circle released and our work complete, I gather us together and speak the word "Tiphareth". This transits us, Swords and all, to the Tiphareth Temple. Here, we will each gently touch our Swords to the central, radiant Diamond, and then place them reverently upon the edge of the pool. Take a good look at your Sword and see how it has been changed by your work with it. It is completely and intimately yours, and yours alone. Remember that henceforth your Sword is only a thought away, safely resting beneath the Diamond in Tiphareth.

At the appropriate moment, I gather us together and we speak the word "Malkuth". This transits us gently downward, through the Yesod Temple to the Malkuth Temple.

After a few moments of re-orientation, I will release the circle casting. Participants will then exit as usual: down the stairs, along the Tunnel, and out the Cave Entrance, ultimately returning to normal physical awareness.

Follow-up Work

As always, write down some notes summarizing your experience.

In the days immediately following your Geburah meditation, go out of your way to do things which promote the manifestation of this aspect of yourself. Nurture what you've set in motion at the subtle Geburian level by providing opportunities for it to manifest at the personal and physical levels of your life. The ultimate effectiveness of the Geburah ritual rests upon how actively you manifest this aspect of yourself in your daily life. In other words, you must consciously bring it down into the highly sequentialized specificity of your current present-moment's now-ness.

Return regularly to the Geburah Temple and explore the full range of your powerfulness. Familiarize yourself thoroughly with the Magical Tools and with the many methods of their use. Make practical use of what you learn and apply it directly to your efforts at self-crafting.

The work in the Gebruah Temple will test you and refine you like a crucible full of metal set in the fire. Each use of your power will teach you how to use it better the next time. You will learn some painful lessons about yourself along the way and will undoubtably, upon occassion, burn your fingers with your own fire. Do not fear this (indeed, in Geburah you will face fear itself and you must overcome it); instead, embrace these instances as opportunities to learn some important lessons.

Your self-crafting efforts must now grow to encompass not only your personality, but your Individuality as well. Examine the Diamond-light of your Individual-self and compare it to the influx of higher light that you perceive coming from within yourself. Note any disparities between the two and seek to self-craft an Individuality that more clearly expresses this influx of higher light. As you make changes in your Individuality, these changes must also be reflected down into your personality and your mundane life circumstance.

This initial self-crafting of the Individuality and consequent re-crafting of the personality, is engaged from within Geburah and is enacted upon Tiphareth.

Gedulah

Introduction

From the Form-pole of Geburah-differentiation, we pass now to the Force-pole of Gedulah-similarity. Gedulah (pronounced "gedd-you-lah") means "greatness, majesty, magnificence" and is therefore associated with the majestically large, gaseous planet Jupiter.

In the Hebrew Tradition, this sphere is also given the title Chesed (pronounced "hess-ed" with a glottal, back of the throat 'h') which means "mercy, compassion, loving kindness". Associated with Gedulah/Chesed is the god-name EL, which translates simply as "god". This EL-god is masculine and singular, unlike the ELOHIM-god whose Hebrew name signifies a mixture of masculine and feminine. EL is, essentially, the masculine, forceful aspect of the ELOHIM.

As the supreme deity of the Olympian pantheon, Jupiter/Zeus is the archetypal symbol of the (mostly) benevolent, fatherly sovereign. This is the Divine Provider, the highest manifestation of the intimately personal, human concept of "god". Which is to say, Jupiter/Zeus stands just below the higher deity forms which are impersonal and universal.

As the non-sequentialized potentials of Binah/Saturn descend into the realm of sequence, the first level of sequentialization they encounter is similarity. Similarity is an attractive Force which binds the Binah-potentials together by virtue of their alikeness and commonality. This primal Force is typified by its qualities of love, mercy, inclusiveness and expansiveness. This sequentialization of the Binah-potentials by virtue of their similarity, causes them to form Individual groupings. At this level though, these Individuals are more united than they are separate -- in Gedulah, separation is a quality defined by degree of alikeness, not by degree of difference.

As we rise upwards, Gedulah marks the most rarified aspect of the Individual-self. Conversely, as the universal Being descends into manifestation, Gedulah marks the most primitive beginnings of Individuation. In Qabbala, Individuation has four basic stages: assimilation, differentiation, expression and personalization. The personalization is represented by the spheres Malkuth, Yesod, Hod and Netzach, through which the Individual-self takes on concrete physical form. The expression is symbolized by the radiant solarity of Tiphareth. The differentiation is symbolized by the exclusivity of Geburah where the Individual learns to constrict its boundaries and define itself by virtue of what it is not. The assimilation is symbolized by Gedulah/Jupiter, for here the Individual is an expansive thing, capable only of inclusiveness.

The ability of our Individual-consciousness to broaden its focus and encompass 'other' within its definition of 'self', is a higher, more potent power than its concurrent ability to bring those boundaries into the sharply limited focus of a physically manifest personal-self. In other words, the primal attractive force of loving kindness -- because it works through alikeness and threads of commonality!!! -- is even more powerful than the secondary repulsive force of severity and differentiation. The power experienced in the Geburah/Mars Temple is as nothing when compared to the power of loving kindness to be experienced in the Gedulah/Jupiter Temple.

In the Western Hermetic Tradition, Jupiter is associated with the major arcana Tarot card, *X: Wheel of Fortune*. This card symbolizes the cyclic force of change, typically called destiny, fortune or luck. In very concrete terms, Gedulah/Jupiter is that finger of change which ceaselessly touches the body of the present-moment.

The force of change (i.e., loving kindness, inclusiveness, expansiveness) works through alikeness. Change/future is always connected, as if by a thread, to the what-has-been/what-is, establishing a certain recognizable continuity of events (i.e., evident causality). The present is related directly to the past by virtue of these threads of commonality/causality upon which change is ceaselessly wrought. Exercising our free will within the confines of our present-moments' now-ness, we can self-consciously establish the what-is and to a great extent determine what threads of commonality are available for change to touch. But, as sequentialized Individuals, we have no power over which among those threads change will actually touch, nor do we have power over how and why change will touch them.

As we each know from personal experience, we have free will to either accept or rebel against the ceaselessness of change. From within the confines of our present-moments' now-ness, we either face forward into that change and meet it gladly, or we look back to our what-has-been and cling to its comforting illusion of changelessness, or we try perhaps to balance ourselves somewhere in between these poles. But whatever we do, we are powerless to alter the fact that change is ceaseless. Even looking back, we are swept forward.

In essence, our *Individual* free will extends only within the limits of our *present-moment* experience of now-ness. The Gedulah/Jupiter force of change is what forms our now-ness, it is what draws our now forward through sequence. Within the confines of our now, our one true power is our innate ability to determine how

102

we ride the ever-cresting wave of change -- our ability to orient ourselves in such a way that change becomes for us a creative, positive, lovingly kind Force. This is our ability to *consciously* move forward *with* our now.

Forwardness to the Individual is the expansion of self, for as the Individual passes through the realm of sequence, it encompasses within itself all the sequence it's passed through. The Individual-self encompasses its past within the now-ness of its present-moment. In other words, the Individual grows. Indeed, growth is a primary expression of the aliveness which typifies all sequentialized Individual things.

The Individual does not die in the same way that the personal- and physical-selves do. The Individual passes through sequence until it matures and comes to encompass the whole infinity of sequence. This encompassing of the whole is a sort of death in that the end is thereby encompassed, but it is the opposite of physical death's finality. It is instead, a passage into all of Life, with a capital 'L'.

Gedulah / Jupiter is the primary manifestation / Individuation of Life and stands right at the lower threshold of the encompassing of the whole. Gedulah receives the descending Binah-potentials and expands with them. In other words, this is the lower side of the interface of the non-sequential and the sequential. Our perspective is from within the realm of sequence and we are looking upwards, perceiving the effects of the Binah-potentials entering our sequentialized realm. We experience this entry as the force of change which defines the forwardness of our present-moment now-ness.

The non-sequentialized Binah-potentials are infinite in number, so from within the realm of sequence, the process of sequentialization is never completed -- its duration is infinite. Thus change (our perception of the Binah-potentials entering our realm of sequence), is ceaseless, for since the Binah-potentials are infinite in number, they will always be descending into the sequential realm.

We sequentialized beings witness the Creation from front-row seats, as it were. The lovingly kind force of change is the Creation, happening in right-now real-time and we are planted smack dab at the center of the action. The Creation doesn't just happen around us, it is happening within us and it is we who are being ceaselessly Created.

Paul Foster Case wrote, in his Pattern on the Trestleboard, statement #4: "From the exhaustless riches of its Limitless Substance, I draw all things needful, both spiritual and material." The infinite number of descending Binah-potentials are the Limitless Substance --

out of which our bubble of now-ness is formed and from which we therefore draw all things needful (a Gedulah/Jupiter process of assimilation, change and growth).

Our Gedulah/Jupiter meditation will focus on Case's statement. We will begin by rising through the six Temples we've already visited. We will do this as if we were putting on a ritual robe. Each Temple/sphere we pass through, we will gather to ourselves and wear as a part of our own bodies.

The figure at right illustrates what we will be doing. Please note that the proper orientation requires a sort of backing-into the Tree of Life symbol. Another way of looking at it, is that you must step into the Tree from behind it and then step off the two-dimensional page, wearing it like a garment.

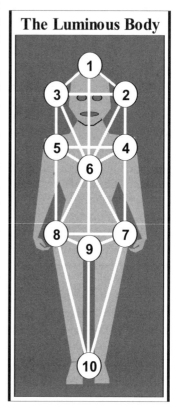

The Luminous Body

As we rise from Malkuth (10) up to Yesod (9), we will visualize Malkuth as a dense, earth-colored sphere and place it at the arches of our feet. We will stand with our feet planted firmly in Malkuth and rise to Yesod.

As we rise from Yesod up-and-over to Hod (8), we will visualize Yesod as a violet sphere and place it at the bottom of our pelvic cavity. Our feet planted in Malkuth and Yesod's glow filling our pelvic cavity, we rise to Hod.

As we rise from Hod over to Netzach (7), we will visualize Hod as an orange sphere and place it at our right hip. With Malkuth at our feet, Yesod at our groin, and Hod permeating our right hip, we rise to Netzach.

As we rise from Netzach up to Tiphareth (6), we will visualize Netzach as an emerald-green sphere and place it at our left hip. With Malkuth at our feet, Yesod at our groin, Hod at our right hip and Netzach permeating our left hip, we rise to Tiphareth.

As we rise from Tiphareth up-and-over to Geburah (5), we will visualize Tiphareth as a radiant golden sun and place it at the center of our chest. With Malkuth at our feet, Yesod at our groin, Hod at our right hip, Netzach at our left hip, and Tiphareth shining at our solar-plexus, we rise to Geburah.

As we rise from Geburah over to Gedulah (4), we will visualize Geburah as a vivid red sphere and place it at our right shoulder. With Malkuth at our feet, Yesod at our groin, Hod at our right hip, Netzach at our left hip, Tiphareth at our solar-plexus, and Geburah permeating our right shoulder, we rise to the Gedulah Temple. Gedulah is brought into this luminous body as a sphere of bright sky-blue and is placed at the left shoulder.

In the Gedulah/Jupiter Temple, we will focus sharply upon what it feels like to be wearing this luminous body. Our visualization will shift to that of the pictured Tiphareth-Diamond and we will con-sciously radiate our Individual Light through the mist of descending Binah-potentials.

Here in Gedulah Temple, these Binah-potentials are symbolized by water. The central fountain and the four corner pillars each emit the Waters of Mercy. The sequentialized cyclicity of the Waters of Mercy cause the appearance of an upper- and a lower-Waters. The four Elemental-poles of the upper-Waters meet to form a great thun-der cloud which rains down upon the lower-Waters and sends down bolts of Life-giving lightning into the atmosphere between these Waters. The lower-Waters spring forth and rise upwards to meet the rain and lightning descending from the upper-Waters. Once met, the homogenous Waters, upper now commingled with lower, fall togeth-er into manifestation.

Standing as radiant Individual Diamond-stars, situated at the point of now-ness where/when the upper- and lower-Waters com-mingle, we will focus upon the rainbow we form within the ever-changing, ever-transient Water vapor. We will draw from this Limitless Substance all things needful to us in our now-ness, and ride consciously with the ever-cresting wave of right-now real-time change. Our focus will be nose-to-nose with the descending infinity of Binah-potentials and we will explore the cutting-edge feel of what it means to be constantly Created . . . to be ceaselessly re-Created.

The spherical rainbow refracted by the vapor of the Waters of Mercy is the equivalent of our luminous bodies. The rainbow demon-strates Individuation-by-similarity, for even though its colors are cre-ated by different spectra of light, it is still a unified, coherent, inter-related whole.

Each color becomes the next color in the sequence by degrees of alikeness -- red passes along the commonality/causality of yellow and by an infinite succession of degrees, it becomes green. The rainbow, like our luminous body, is one of an infinite number of Individual microcosmic manifestations of the macrocosm. An Individual micro-cosmic body directly mirrors the overall structure of the macrocosm, but it does not contain the whole infinity of possibilities encompassed by macro-cosm.

Our Gedulah Temple meditation will end with a simple ritual of "high magic" -- we will consciously descend into our luminous body, consciously filling it and causing it to be. As we return to Malkuth we will be wrapping ourselves in this garment and forming with it our daily life circumstances. It is "high magic" because our daily life is in fact, the present-moment, real-time, highly sequentialized manifesta-tion of our luminous body.

MEDITATION #7: GEDULAH

Begin as usual: pass through the Cave Entrance, along the Tunnel passage, up the ten steps, and into the Malkuth Temple where I stand awaiting your arrival.

When all the participants have arrived, I will gather us together and cast a ritual circle.

Once our circle is cast, we will spend several moments together in the center of the Malkuth Temple, holding hands in a circle and bringing our awareness of the presences of the other participants into focus. As you look around the circle, try to sense the unique presence of each participant.

At the appropriate moment, I will bring our focus to the East quarter altar -- our gateway to Gedulah. Upon the altar, we see the square fountain of the Waters of Mercy. Standing within this spray of Water is the radiant, central Diamond from the Tiphareth Temple.

Behind the altar, we see the same curtain and symbol we encounter at the Cave Entrance.

As I light the candles upon the altar, we speak, as with a single voice, the phrase: "El, please guide me to Gedulah."

In answer to our prayer, the Hebrew letters אל (AL) appear near the top of the curtain, as if written with light.

The upward pointing white triangle shines forth, as does the middle sphere on the right-hand pillar, and a soft light glows behind the curtain.

When we see this illumination, I reach forward and draw the curtain aside.

This reveals a realm of purest, upwardly rushing Water and we are swept up by it. We rush upwards to Yesod, remembering to form our Malkuth-sphere at the arches of our feet.

Briefly we are aware of our passage through the Yesod Temple as we are swept towards Hod. We picture Malkuth at our feet and add a Yesod-sphere at our groin.

As we pass from Hod to Netzach, we add a Hod-sphere at our right hip. Passing still upwards, we add a Netzach-sphere at our left hip, then a Tiphareth-sphere at our solar plexus, and then a Geburah-sphere at our right shoulder. This brings us into the Gedulah Temple and we add a Gedulah-sphere at our left shoulder. When we have all arrived in the Gedulah Temple, we will pause for a few moments of orientation . . .

At the appropriate moment, I will bring our circle together and we will focus sharply upon the presences of the other Individual participants. Notice the subtle differences which distinguish one Individual from another and then pointedly shift your attention to the similarities which render each recognizable as an Individual. See how the luminous body of one (though Individually unique) is alike the luminous body of each of the others.

Next we will look just as sharply within ourselves. Turn your attention inward and sense, as deeply as possible, what it feels like for you to wear your luminous body. Flow along the commonality /causality thread of your luminous body's radiance and merge with your Tiphareth-Diamond self. Stand, as illustrated, at the meeting place where the upper- and lower-Waters commingle.

We will then spend several minutes in private meditation upon Paul Case's statement #4: "From the exhaustless riches of its Limitless Substance, I draw all things needful, both spiritual and material." Try, as you meditate, to place yourself firmly in the present-moment now-ness. From within that now-ness, face directly into the ever-cresting wave of change and try your best to reorient yourself so that instead of it washing over you, you wash down with it. Seek out your place within the ever-cresting wave of change and flow with it.

Feel yourself as a radiant being, stationed precisely at that point in time-space where/when the future penetrates the present. As you

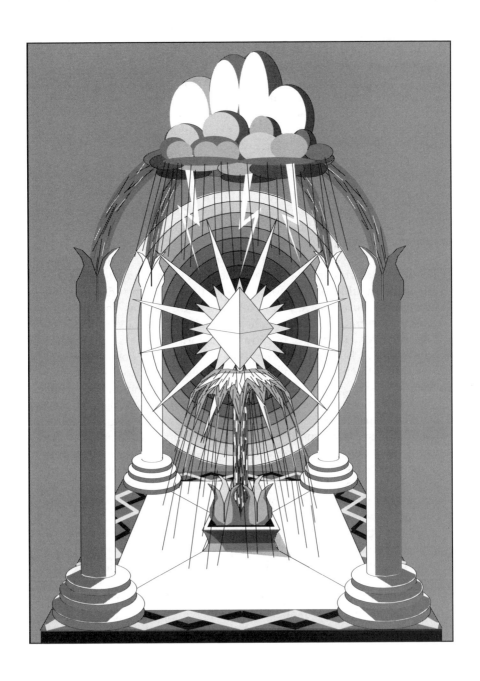

radiate into the ever-changing, ever-new Limitless Substance of Water vapor, draw from it what is needful to the ceaseless reCreation of your luminous body. Observe the threads of commonality/causality which sustain the continuity of your luminous body. Though it exists within the medium of ever-newness and is ceaselessly reCreated, it still manifests a specific continuity -- it is continuously this thing you recognize as your luminous body.

Examine, explore and learn by direct experience all that you can of this realm of ever-new now-ness.

At the appropriate moment I will bring our focus together and we will begin the ritual of conscious descent into Malkuth. I utter the word Gedulah and sphere 4 of our luminous bodies shines forth strongly at the left shoulder.

I utter the word Geburah and we are transited to the Geburah Temple. We bring our Gedulah bodies into Geburah and sphere 5 at our right shoulder shines forth. Take a moment to sense how the power of Geburah, since you've touched Gedulah, now has about it a sense of inspiration. See how the Gedulah force of Loving Kindness fills and gives a nobility of purpose to the form of your Geburian powerfulness. Let Loving Kindness permeate all of your powerfulness.

I utter the word Tiphareth and we are transited to the Tiphareth Temple. As before, we bring our higher Gedulah-Geburah bodies into Tiphareth and sphere 6 becomes a radiant sun which fills our chest cavities. Sense how the quality of your radiations are changed by the Gedulah-inspiration and the inspired Geburah-powerfulness.

I utter the word Netzach and our Gedulah-Geburah-Tiphareth bodies are transited to the Netzach Temple. As sphere 7 shines forth at your left hip, sense how your emotional realm is changed and matured to a higher nobility by your having brought your higher body consciously down into it.

I utter the word Hod and we are transited to the Hod Temple. As sphere 8 shines forth at your right hip, sense how the presence of your higher body refines and clarifies your powers of intellection and reason.

I utter the word Yesod and we are transited to the Yesod Temple. As sphere 9 shines forth and fills your pelvic cavity, sense how your higher body coalesces and becomes the coherent personality you manifest.

I utter the word Malkuth and our Gedulah-Geburah-Tiphareth-Netzach-Hod-Yesod bodies transit gently to the Malkuth Temple. Sphere 10 forms itself solidly at our feet and we stand firmly planted upon it. We stand, wearing our whole luminous body in Malkuth. Sense what wearing your luminous body in Malkuth feels like for you personally.

We will close with a short meditation on Paul Case's statement #10: "The Kingdom of Spirit is embodied in my flesh."

At the appropriate moment, I will draw us together and, holding hands, luminous body joined to luminous body in a circle, we will offer up our prayers of thanks. Then I will release the circle casting and we will bid our goodbyes.

As you leave the Malkuth Temple, do so with great self-consciousness. Concentrate upon your luminous body and consciously move with it, down the stairs, through the tunnel and out the Cave entrance. Take the awareness and sensation of your luminous body with you as you return to normal physical awareness. When you are firmly back into your physical body, take a few minutes more to yourself and visualize your luminous body surrounding and permeating you. As you get up and go about your business, try to keep this awareness of your luminous body with you for as long as you can.

Follow-up Work

As always, write down some notes summarizing your experience.

In the days immediately following your Gedulah meditation, take time periodically to visualize your luminous body. Remember to wear it and while wearing it, examine those threads of commonality / causality which connect your luminous body to the circumstances of your daily life. Acquaint yourself thoroughly with your luminous body.

Don't hesitate to project your personal shield if working with your luminous body makes you feel at all vulnerable. Your shield and your luminous body are quite compatible and the one will augment the other.

Return regularly to the Gedulah Temple and pursue there the work of fine tuning the self-crafting of your Individuality. Thoroughly familiarize yourself with the now and with the threads of causality connecting past with future. Set your imagination free and experiment with the manipulation of those threads of causality.

Working directly with the causal threads that permeate and sustain the universe is a very high form of magic called "Causality Magic". Only an Individual who is well along the path of self-crafting and who has truly learned the lessons of Geburah, is allowed access to this high a magic. In other words, one is led to this higher ability only by successfully passing through the lessons of Geburah -- there is no other entry than that, for there is no such thing as a short cut to the higher magics!

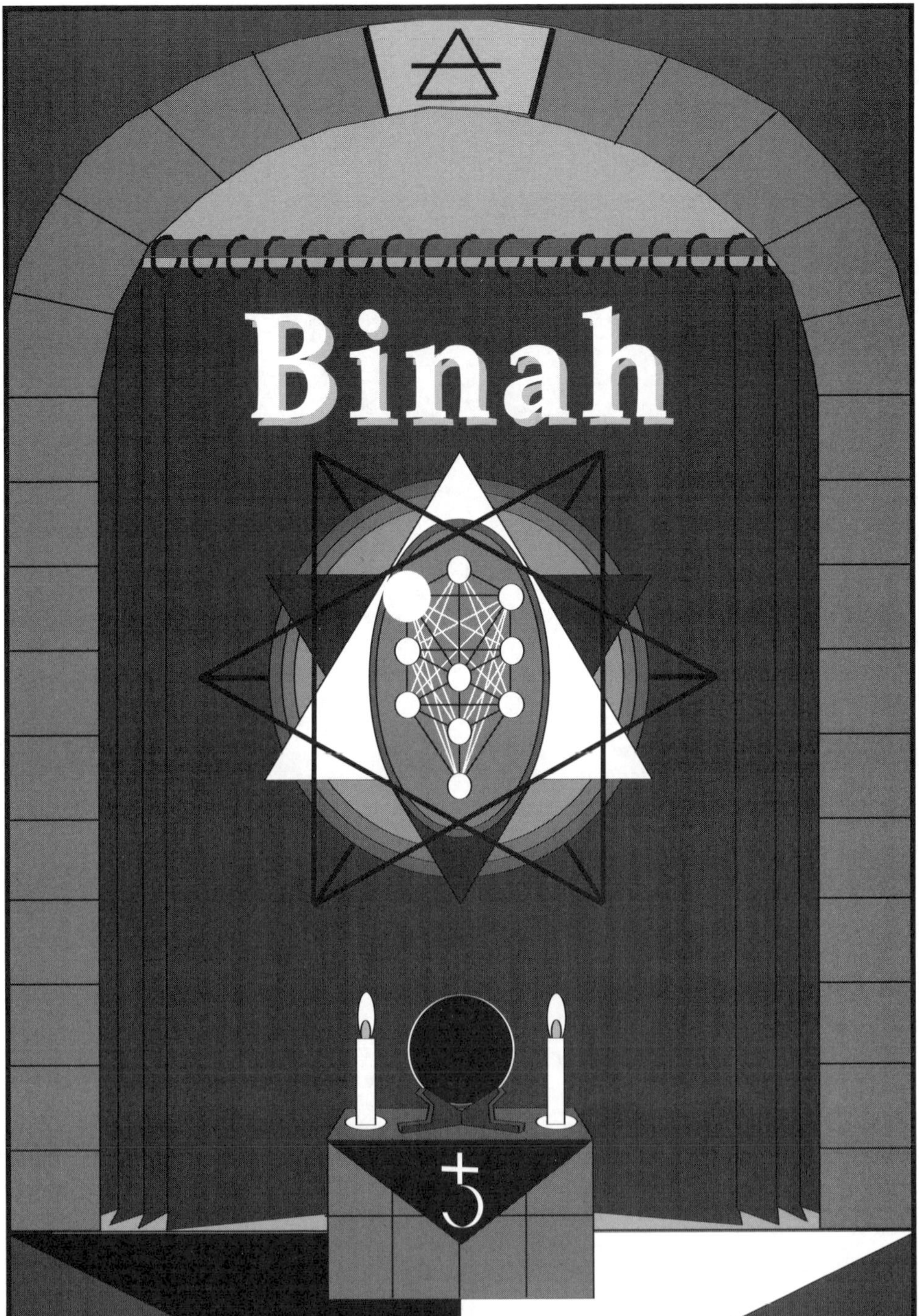
Binah

Introduction

Prior to our modern, scientific age, our conception of the cosmos was derived from direct observation of the night sky by the unaided human eye. To those seeking to understand it, the cosmos was a Divine thing whose observable phenomena reflected the mysterious "body" or structure of deity. But due to the lack of more advanced scientific apparatus, assumptions were made by those early observers that today we would laugh at. Nonetheless, the astrological symbolism we use today stems directly from that ancient age of symbol-knowledge.

Up until the late 1700's, Saturn was known as the outermost planet of our solar system. The ancients thought that beyond Saturn there was an "abyss" -- an empty, dark region in which there were no other "planets". On the other side of this "abyss" there was thought to be another order of existence symbolized by the "fixed stars" of the zodiacal constellations. And beyond Saturn, beyond the abyss, and beyond even the celestial zodiac, the ancients thought that there lay an utterly unknowable realm -- the infinite blackness of space itself.

When we think of the universe in this modern day, we know for certain that Saturn is not the outermost planet and we know that there are other planets surrounding the stars that make up our familiar constellations. Distance seems the only "abyss" between us and those other realms.

To us, the universe is an astrophysical phenomenon, a rational and ultimately understandable occurrence; but to the ancients, the universe was

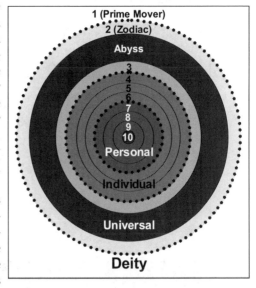

a symbol of the Divine. So, for our modern minds to understand the meaning of symbol-Saturn, we have to let go of our modern scientific-knowledge of the universe and surround ourselves instead with the ancient's symbolic-knowledge.

The Roman god Saturn (Greek god Kronos) is "Father Time", the great limiter. He is a "father" to symbolize that he is a conduit for the Celestial Seed. In other words, the realm of Saturn focuses the celestial influences of the zodiac into the lower realms symbolized by the planets. He also confers mortality, allotting a specific duration of time to each thing within his realm of influence. His focus is sun-ward -- downward and inward, toward his planetary offspring. As the interface of the universal and the personal, he is at once strict and compassionate, unrelenting yet considerate.

The Hebrews (and much of the rest of the world) however, characterized Saturn as female instead of male and gave it the name "Shabbatai". This word means "peace, rest, cessation" and is derived from the same root as the word "Sabbath". Thus Saturn/Shabbatai is associated with the 7th day of Creation -- the Sabbath, which for the Jews occurs on the day we call Saturday (Saturn's day).

The true depth of the Hebrew symbolism is found in Saturn/Shabbatai's association with the sphere of Binah (pronounced "Bee-nuh") which translates as "understanding". In the Hebrew system, Binah/Saturn is placed on the far side of the "abyss", and is therefore less personal than the Roman god Saturn.

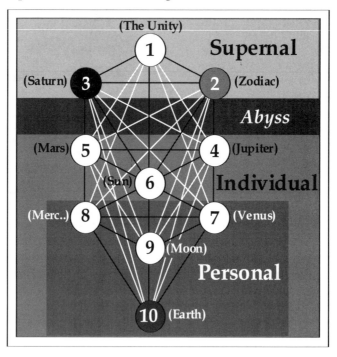

Binah, instead of being a masculine seed, is a female womb. She carries and gives form to the Celestial seed, passing it to lower realms in that way.

Here, the masculine aspects are encompassed by the feminine. In other words, Binah carries within her the same aspects we saw in masculine Saturn/Kronos, but she sets those aspects into a slightly different context.

Binah is called the "Mother". She is said to have two faces: the "Dark Sterile Mother" and the "Bright Fertile Mother". In essence, the "Dark Sterile Mother" is the limiting-Binah that we see as we raise our consciousness upward. It defines the limits of being as we humans know it and marks the edge of a realm foreign to our normal experience of things. This is how Binah appears to us when our perspective is from below the "abyss", looking upwards.

The "Bright Fertile Mother" on the other hand, is what Binah looks like when we have crossed the "abyss" and are looking downwards. From this perspective, one sees that the Divine Seed fills Binah and is given form, and that it ceaselessly passes down into the realm of sequence.

The duality implied by these titles connects us back to the earlier conception of the cosmos which places a personal-Saturn on the near side of the "abyss" -- instead of placing a universal-Saturn on the far side of the "abyss" as do the Qabbalists. In practice, Binah/Saturn straddles the "abyss" and exists on both of its sides. The lower manifestation of Binah is only an appearance, a dark reflection of the upper Binah, but it is, nonetheless, what leads us across the "abyss" to that higher Binah.

Despite the image it elicits, the "abyss" is not a spatial thing. It is called by this specifically spatial word because that is our nearest human corollary. What it symbolizes is the experiential gulf separating the sequential and non-sequential realms. To the rising human consciousness, it appears to be vast and empty because we have no frame of reference to understand what lies within and beyond it. It is dark because our sequentialized consciousness is not capable of perceiving the non-sequential Light.

Rising from the sequential realm of Individualized conscious to the non-sequential realm is called "crossing the abyss". This crossing requires a radical shift of experiential perspective. This shift concerns four essential, intimately related categories of experience:

#1) Type of Consciousness. Despite what grand things we think of ourselves, humanoid consciousness is only one type of consciousness in a universe filled by an infinite number of different types of consciousness. The differentiation of consciousness into types is an aspect of sequentialization. Crossing the abyss therefore, requires a letting go of the specifically human limitation of consciousness, and a merging with the infinitude of other, non-humanoid types of consciousness.

As other types are experienced, the boundaries of the human consciousness expand to include a broader range of perspectives. Eventually the differences blur and the underlying commonality of consciousness itself leads one to merge with its infinite wholeness.

The simultaneous experience of the whole infinity of types of consciousness, human and non-human, is what is meant by the phrase "become more than human". Ultimately, it is a non-sequential experience, or rather, it is an experience of the non-sequential realm. Though it may take the average human quite a long sequence of experiences to achieve, the ultimate encompassing-of-the-whole happens all at once, in a single quantum leap, as it were.

There are many exercises which can aid one in achieving this shift, specifically those having to do with transference of consciousness. This is a meditational technique where one first isolates one's own consciousness and then sends it out into another object or creature. In other words, one transfers one's consciousness into the other thing and seeks to merge with the other thing's experience of consciousness.

For example, if you wanted to experience what a specific tree experiences and perceive the universe as that tree perceives it, you would transfer your conscious awareness into the body of the tree and then try to merge your consciousness with its consciousness. At first you will experience the tree from a human perspective, but as you let go of the differentiation which separates your human-ness from the tree's tree-ness, your awareness will naturally follow the lines of commonality and merge with that of the tree itself. The difference between experiencing the tree from a human perspective and from a perspective that is truly merged with that of the tree itself, is unmistakable -- you will know it when you experience it!

The same technique may be applied to any object or creature at hand. It is important --for both your own well-being and for any chance at success -- that you approach this sort of work with a deep, deep respect and reverence for life and for the sovereignty and privacy of others! If your actions are invasive or abusive, you will pay a steep karmic price. You must guide yourself by a strict code of personal ethics and never stray from it.

#2) Time-Space. Time and space are manifestations of sequentialization. In the non-sequential realm, consciousness experiences the whole passage of sequence -- physical, astral and mental time-space -- within a singular, all-inclusive now. At this level, consciousness pervades everything and experiences everything simultaneously. There is certainly a cognizance of sequentiality, but there is not a direct sequential involvement with it.

An illustration can be drawn from the human body: Our conscious awareness pervades our physical body and causes it to be, but is not intimately involved in the functions of all of the body's various organs. Likewise, the non-sequential pervades the sequential realm and causes it to be, but is not directly involved with the enacting of each moment in that infinite sequence.

This is not to say that that the non-sequential consciousness cannot reach down into the realm of sequence and directly experience its minutia, for quite the contrary is true. The non-sequential consciousness however, ceases to be non-sequential when it reaches down into the realm of sequence. In fact, the realm of sequence is nothing other than the reaching down of non-sequential consciousness -- it is this reaching down which causes sequentialization, and it is non-sequential consciousness which is itself sequentialized. In other words, the sequential realm is the body of the non-sequential.

Crossing the abyss requires that one step out of direct involvement in the minutia of time-space-sequence. This stepping out follows the lines of commonality which unite the two realms. The macrocosmic thread of causality which concerns the shift in time-space perspective is that of now-ness. The quality of now-ness is the same for a sequentialized consciousness as it is for the non-sequential consciousness. The only difference between these experiences of now-ness is in their quantity. The quantity of the sequentialized now, is infinitely small and the quantity of the non-sequential now is infinitely large, but they both share the same essential quality of now-ness.

In short, the experience of now-ness is the doorway through which one steps and the pathway one follows across the abyss. Meditations and experiences which increase your understanding of now-ness are helpful in this process. Specifically those which increase the quantity of your now.

#3) Definition of Self. We have seen and directly experienced in the seven previous meditations that there are several levels of Self. At the physical, personal and Individual levels that we have explored, there has always been a sense of our essential I-ness. By I-ness, I mean that sense of autonomous, sovereign self we all have in common though we experience it, each in our own unique ways.

The I-ness we experience at the physical and personal levels of self has the same quality as that of the Individual self, but is of a smaller quantity. The Individual self truly encompasses the experiences of many, many personal and physical incarnations and so its sense of I-ness is of a larger quantity, but it is, nonetheless, of the same quality.

Crossing the abyss between our sequentialized experience of I-ness (tied directly to our experience of now-ness!) and a non-sequential experience of I-ness is very similar to the aforementioned shift in time-space perspective. There is a similar stepping out of direct involvement with the minutia of sequentialized I-ness and one follows the line of commonality established by the quality of I-ness shared by every level of consciousness.

Here, meditations which increase the quantity of your experience of I-ness are most helpful. First are meditations which lead to the recovery of the storehouse of the Individual's memory of all its incarnations. This expands the quantity of the Individual's I-ness to its maximum. Next come meditations which unite the Individual's I-ness with that of other Individuals of a human-type consciousness. This results in awareness and I-ness which encompasses many Individuals simultaneously. These follow lines of commonality and together, that number of connected Individuals constitute what I call a "Greater Self". There is still the same quality of I-ness , but the quantity of the I-ness is expanded by a significant order of magnitude. Eventually the humanoid Greater Selves unite with the infinite number of other Greater Selves and experience the true Unity of Being.

Actually that last sentence is incorrect in that it conveys the idea that the experience is sequential. Unfortunately, these sequential words and our sequential process called thinking, both preclude the possibility of accurately describing a non-sequential experience! To describe it, I must sequentialize it and present in in a specific order, but the experience itself happens without order and sequence.

When the I-ness of the humanoid Greater Self is experienced (symbolized here by Binah/Saturn), one simultaneously unites with all the non-humanoid Greaters and becomes directly cognizant of the Unity. The Unity shares the same essential quality of I-ness as every one of Its manifestations, but Its quantity of I-ness is infinite.

#4) Thinking. Thought, as we know it, is a sequential process. But in the non-sequential realm consciousness does not think sequentially. There, instead of one thought following another thought, all thoughts exist together and without separation. The non-sequential consciousness therefore experiences the entire infinity of thought as a unified whole.

Crossing the abyss requires that one let go of sequentialized thinking altogether. Deep meditations upon the nature of mind and upon the processes of thought are therefore helpful.

Truly, it is impossible to satisfactorily describe the non-sequential realm. I fear that continuing the attempt would only add further confusion. All I can say is that it's best to look for yourself and only then will you truly understand -- hence the Hebrew title of this sphere, Binah / Understanding.

Paul Case wrote, regarding Binah/Saturn: "#3) Filled with Understanding of its perfect law, I am guided, moment by moment, along the path of liberation." The guidance he speaks of here is a very real thing! Quite simply, our guide is our own Greater Self. This guide speaks to our inner ear with the voice of our own conscience and subtly guides us through every moment of our sequentialized existence.

Our Binah/Saturn meditation is designed to simulate several aspects of the actual abyss crossing. Our Temple this time, has two parts. The first part symbolizes the lower Binah and what a sequentialized consciousness can understand of it; thus it is stationed below the abyss. The second part symbolizes the upper Binah and the non-sequential realm itself.

Our journey from the Malkuth Temple to the first part of our Binah Temple, will be a passage through utter darkness. The first part of the Binah Temple is constructed from very simple symbols. You will recognize three of the four pillars from the Gedulah Temple. One casts no shadow and is completely white; one casts a gray shadow; and one casts a black shadow. These three pillars stand upon a set of three triangular slabs: one black, one gray, and one white.

At the center of the first part of our Binah Temple, there sits a large black sphere, resting upon a gray tripod. This sphere is both utterly black and at the same time radiant -- it is the source of the light which causes the pillar's gray and black shadows. This black sphere symbolizes our direct connection to the guidance of our Greater Self. Therefore a portion of our meditation will be spent communing, through this sphere, with our own personal guide.

A dark realm surrounds the first part of our Binah Temple. The Temple itself sits right at the edge of a great, utterly black ocean. This ocean represents the abyss which we will symbolically cross.

The abyss is infinite. This means that at a very practical level there is only one way to cross it. Many have tried swim across, boat across, fly across, and even walk across; but due to the infinite breadth of the abyss, these options take, quite literally, forever. The only way to cross an infinity is to become the infinity. In other words, the way across the abyss is to merge with the abyss.

To facilitate your experience of the abyss, I have chosen to use the symbolism of water. In this infinite black ocean, there is no differentiation. Each molecule of water is the same as every other molecule. Within this ocean the potential for differentiation is everywhere present. Here are all the ingredients for life, but they are not placed into sequence and thus exist here in a formless, seemingly chaotic state.

After a time of communing with our Greater Self through the black sphere, we will enter the ocean of infinite blackness and cross it by merging our consciousness with it. Using the water symbolism, we each enter the ocean as a distinct current of water which eventually becomes an homogenous part of the whole ocean. Each of the four categories of experience mentioned above can be related to this water symbolism:

#1) Type of consciousness. Begin by focusing upon your own type of water -- that which distinguishes you as a specific current. Follow the lines of commonality between your current and the homogenous ocean of water.

#2) Time-space. Begin by focusing upon your own experience of now-ness -- both its quality and its quantity. Follow the lines of commonality between your small quantity of now and the quantity of now symbolized by the infinite ocean. The quality of now-ness is your connection to the homogeneity of the ocean, for it is shared by every one of its molecules simultaneously.

#3) Definition of Self. Begin by focusing upon your own sense of I-ness, both its quality and quantity. Follow the lines of commonality established by the quality of I-ness and merge your I-ness with the water which immediately surrounds you. Keep expanding the parameters of your I-ness and increase its quantity till you have merged with the whole ocean of I-ness. The idea here is to expand your definition of Self till you feel and experience that you are the whole ocean. At that moment, there is no 'other', there is only I.

#4) Thinking. Begin by recognizing that you are thinking and that you are experiencing things sequentially. One evidence of this is the fact that you are seeing visual symbols. These symbols are a part of your sequentialized thought process. The line of commonality connecting sequential thought to non-sequential consciousness is essential meaning. In other words, follow the essential meaning behind your thoughts and behind the symbols you encounter, and simultaneously let go of their sequentialized forms. Use the undifferentiated blackness of the ocean's water to support this letting go. Let your eyes rest in its pure blackness and its lack of visual symbols. And in a similar manner, let its homogeneity rest your mind from differentiated thought entirely.

For the purposes of this meditation, I suggest you pursue whichever line of commonality is the easiest for you to follow. Once you have succeeded by whatever means (and to whatever degree) in merging your consciousness with this symbolic ocean of infinite potential, try to sense its opposite shore. Then try to locate the second part of our Binah Temple which lies upon that far shore.

The environment surrounding the second part of our Binah Temple is noticeably brighter. Just like the first part, the second part of the Temple is very simple. You will notice that some of the black and white polarities have been reversed. Most importantly, the sphere at the center of the second part of the Temple is white instead of black.

When the opposite shore is sensed and the second part of the Temple located, we will then step out of the abyssal ocean and stand before the white sphere. This stepping out of the ocean is radically different from our initial stepping into the ocean. When we step out of it, we step out as the ocean. We do not step out as differentiated, sequentialized parts of the ocean. In other words, it is as your all-encompassing Greater Self that you stand before the white sphere.

Within the white sphere you will be able to view the entire infinite realm of sequence. It appears from beginning to end simultaneously and you experience it within a singular now and with the knowledge that it is encompassed within your singular I.

We will take the opportunity to look into the white sphere and cast our consciousness far enough into the realm of sequence for us to see the Individual Self we are "currently" manifesting. Similar to our Tiphareth Meditation, we will gaze down at our Individual, personal and physical selves. From Binah however, this vision is not of a singular incarnation, but of a nearly infinite number Individual manifestations, each with their personal and physical incarnations.

Our meditation will conclude with the identification of our "current", familiar Individualities and we will each descend into the Tiphareth Temple and consciously inhabit our Individual Selves. Then we will descend through Yesod to the Malkuth Temple.

Since this is the last in our series of eight meditations, I will close with a short blessing ritual in the Malkuth Temple, celebrating the culmination of our work.

MEDITATION #8: BINAH

Begin as usual: pass through the Cave Entrance, along the Tunnel passage, up the ten steps, and into the Malkuth Temple where I stand awaiting your arrival.

When all the participants have arrived, I will gather us together and cast a ritual circle.

Once our circle is cast, we will spend several moments together in the center of the Malkuth Temple, holding hands in a circle and bringing our awareness of the presences of the other participants into focus. As you look around the circle, try to sense the unique presence of each participant.

At the appropriate moment, I will bring our focus to the East quarter altar -- our gateway to Binah. Upon the altar, we see an obsidian black sphere, resting on a small tripod.

Behind the altar, we see the same curtain and symbol we encounter at the Cave Entrance.

As I light the candles upon the altar, we speak, as with a single voice, the phrase: "I-H-V-H Elohim (pronounced "yawd-hay-vawv-hay eh-low-heem"), please guide me to Binah."

In answer to our prayer, the Hebrew letters יהוה אלהים (IHVH ALHIM) appear near the top of the curtain, as if written with light. The upward pointing white triangle shines forth, as does the topmost sphere on the left-hand pillar, and a soft light glows behind the curtain.

When we see this illumination, I reach forward and draw the curtain aside. This reveals a realm of utter darkness -- a complete blackness that is, somehow, also radiant. I gather together the radiance of this darkness and hold it aloft like a lantern to light our way.

The lantern illumines only the darkness immediately surrounding us and reveals no details within the seemingly infinite darkness. We step together through the archway and into the darkness, and are led blindly forward by our lantern's meager illumination.

As we move through the darkness, we shed our physical and astral bodies, travelling eventually with only our mental bodies. The darkness has a timelessness to it, but finally we reach the first part of our Binah Temple.

After a moment of orientation, I will direct our awareness to the Temple's central black sphere. We will then spend several minutes communing with the guidance radiating from the sphere.

At the appropriate moment, I will turn our attention to the ocean

126

of blackness. We will then descend the Temple's three steps and enter the dark water. Several minutes will be devoted to the process of merging with this infinite ocean.

At the appropriate moment, I will direct your attention to the opposite shore and the second part of our Binah Temple. As you arise from the ocean, do your best to arise as the ocean and stand before the Temple's central white sphere.

We will spend several minutes gazing into this sphere. At first, we will examine the sequential realm in its wholeness. Then we will gaze into the sphere and locate our Individual manifestations.

At the appropriate moment, I will utter the word Tiphareth. This gently transits us along the lines of causality which tie our Greater Selves to our "current" Individualities. We consciously descend into the realm of sequence and find ourselves standing together in our familiar Tiphareth Temple. Take a moment at this juncture to fully sense your familiar Individual Self and review its connection to your Greater Self.

I will then utter the words Yesod and Malkuth. As we transit from Tiphareth, through Yesod, to Malkuth, concentrate upon consciously inhabiting your personal self. Fully sense your familiar personality and life circumstance, and review its connection to your Individual and Greater Selves.

At the appropriate moment, I will gather us together in the Malkuth Temple for a short blessing ritual. During this time, please focus upon your luminous body of spheres. Visualize Malkuth as an earthy colored sphere at the arches of your feet; Yesod as a violet sphere filling your pelvic cavity; Hod as an orange sphere at your right hip; Netzach as an emerald green sphere at your left hip; Tiphareth as a yellow sun filling your chest; Geburah as a red sphere at your right shoulder; and, Gedulah as a blue sphere at your left shoulder. Now add Binah/Saturn as a black sphere at your right temple and let its radiance permeate the right hemisphere of your brain. To finish, we will add a gray sphere at the left temple and a sphere of white brilliance at the crown. This completes the luminous body and concludes our meditation series.

We will close with a group prayer of thanks. Then I will release the circle casting and we will bid our goodbyes.

As you leave the Malkuth Temple, try to remain aware of your luminous body and of your connection to your Greater Self. When you have completed your return to your physical body, take a few more moments of quiet time to fully sense your luminous body and to once again reaffirm your connection to your Greater Self. Then consciously and fully return to your normal waking consciousness. This may take some internal down-shifting, as it were, but it is important that you return to a normal state after each contact with your Greater Self.

Follow-up Work

As always, write down some notes summarizing your experience.

In the days immediately following your Binah meditation, review your experiences with your Greater Self and listen closely for the guiding voice of your conscience. When you interact with others, consciously allow your awareness of your connection with all things to permeate and bless your interaction.

Return regularly to the Binah Temple for further explorations of the Abyss. The true crossing is an accomplishment that takes lifetimes to perfect. This is not, by any means, to say that you will not achieve it in your present lifetime. Rather, it says "take heart!" For depending upon your efforts in past lifetimes and, most especially, upon your efforts in your present life, anything is possible.

Oddly enough, when the time is right, you will succeed in truly crossing the Abyss. Time's rightness however, is something you have a certain amount of power to effect. The process of self-crafting and the pursuit of the meditations regarding your human-ness, your now-ness, I-ness, and sequentialized thinking, will all help to mature your time to ripeness. But ultimately, the timing of your crossing is not within your Individual control -- it is only when the universe concurs that time then reaches its true rightness.

This is a process unique to each person. There is no external guidance available -- only that provided internally, by your own Greater Self. It is essential therefore, that you develop the discipline of obedience to your conscience, for it is the voice of your Greater Self. By following its dictates, you will deepen your contact with your true guide and it will never fail you.

Be sure to ground yourself thoroughly back into your normal waking consciousness when you are through with each meditation on the Abyss. Experiences of the non-sequential realm take time (sequence!) to fully integrate themselves into your life, so patience, conscientiousness and care are recommended in this regard.

EPILOGUE

In the four years that have passed between the original creation of the Eight Temples Meditation Project and the publication of this little book, well over 100 people (that I'm aware of) have pursued these meditation rituals. Many of them have written to me, describing their experiences or asking for clarification. For me, this exchange has been educational and I would like to share with you some of the things I've learned from those who have since done this work.

The most frequently asked question has concerned the level of ability necessary to pursue this work. The answer is simply, none. Of the original participants, I alone was the only trained magician. And of the many that have pursued the Project since, only a minority have had any significant training. The only prerequisite is a desire to participate in this work and the only faculty you'll need is your creative imagination.

This has been a special concern for students of Franz Bardon's "Initiation Into Hermetics". Many are leery of entering into a side practice that would jeopardize their progress, and rightly so, but the Eight Temples in no way presents a conflict. In fact, I designed the Project with this specifically in mind and created it as a compliment to the work of "Initiation Into Hermetics". The Project especially supports the work of self-analysis and subsequent self-transformation that forms the heart of initiation.

Another common question has been whether or not a participant must have prior knowledge of qabbalah. While it certainly doesn't hurt, it is not necessary. The qabbalistic terminology is not crucial to the successful pursuit of this Project and each of the terms I do use is explained.

Not long ago, I was discussing with a friend the difficulty of deciding which book to suggest as a bare-bones introduction to qabbalah for the beginner (a question I'm frequently asked). To my great surprise, this friend replied, "Well, the Eight Temples Project, of course!" He went on to say that out of all the books he'd read on the subject, the Eight Temples was the most helpful because it was *experiential*. It didn't just fill his mind with a bunch of difficult terms and complex concepts and then leave it at that. Instead, it presented him with an opportunity to *experience* qabbalah as a living, breathing, useful thing.

Until that moment, I hadn't seen the Project in this light, but now I see the wisdom of his words. In the time since that conversation, I've conferred with a couple of the original participants and asked what they thought of the Project as an introduction to qabbalah. Since neither had much knowledge of qabbalah prior to the Project, they both claim that the Project *was* their introduction to qabbalah! Their experience with the Project not only introduced them to qabbalah, it also ignited a sincere interest in qabbalah that thrives to this day.

I've also taken the opportunity to review the correspondence I've received from subsequent participants and it's evident that the same has held true for the majority of them. It appears that the Project serves as an excellent, *experiential* introduction to qabbalistic concepts.

Perhaps the third most commonly asked question is whether or not the entire script of each meditation ritual needs to be memorized. The answer is no, the entire script does not need to be memorized, but the salient points do. It is especially important that you memorize the sequence of events so that you don't have to refer back to the script in the middle of the meditation ritual.

It is equally important that you visualize each event. For instance, when the Hebrew letters are scripted to appear at the top of the archway curtain, it is vital that you visualize this occurring. Or when it is scripted for me to cast the ritual circle, you should visualize my doing so. [For a description of a circle casting, please refer to the Geburah meditation ritual.]

You should also spend ample time beforehand, reading through the introductory material and memorizing the Temple and Altar images for each meditation ritual.

Another important issue that has arisen (this one from participant's experiences, instead of their questions) has to do with when is the best time to perform the meditation rituals. While it was absolutely necessary for their creation to occur in sync with the Full Moon, it has proven to be far better if they are performed in sync with the New Moon. Generally, this is a time of introspection which is much more conducive for your initial working of each meditation ritual.

As you read through the Project, it is apparent that even though it was designed as an eight month course, it can well become a life's work. What I suggest is that you perform all eight meditation rituals, one per month on each New Moon, for eight months in a row. Then, after you've been introduced to all eight Temples, go back and independently pursue the work of each Temple to its fullest. This is where the Temples manifest their greatest value - with the self-directed, in-depth work.

I await you in the Eight Temples!

Rawn Clark

(May 2002)

Appendix

Beneath

an Astral Moon

Introduction

An e-mail discussion group with the topic of "Hermetic Philosophy", was the setting in which I encountered K. Despite living hundreds of miles apart, we became fast friends and began an e-mail correspondence which thrives to this day.

In early November of 1995, my friend K proposed that we begin a magical project together. He spoke of building "the Astral Temple, where one may repair to Work." He said, "What does it matter that we are separated by mere miles? Let's collect a merry band, from the far corners of netdom if need be, and put together the 'coven' we've all been waiting for! What do you think?"

I took to the idea immediately!

Our first step was to discuss and clarify the parameters of our project. Why were we going to do this? How were we going to do this? What is our goal?

From these and other questions, we concluded that this was an "experiment". Our primary goal was to achieve a "shared astral experience". Even though we held hopes that "shared" might mean jointly experiencing exactly the same visual, acoustic and tactile details; we still resolved to, as much as possible, set aside these and other preconceptions, and approach this project in the true spirit of experimentation.

We agreed to establish an astral locale and to meet there together. After each meeting, we would independently write a report describing our own experiences, and then e-mail them to each other.

Throughout November and most of December, 1995, we went about establishing our astral locale. It came naturally to us both to visualize an outdoor setting, and for a little over a month we traveled there separately, each conducting our independent explorations. We reported our individual impressions of the place via e-mail, but did not meet there together till the night of December 21st, 1995 -- New Moon, followed by the Winter Solstice.

Six months and a dozen joint meetings later, having learned countless lessons along the way and having realized our most basic goals, we opened our experiment to include a third person ("V"). Another six months of meetings and even more lessons later, we were back down to two.

Marking our first anniversary of astral meetings, we resolved to open our experiment again; so in January of 1997, we included a new third-person ("T"). This was so successful that we opened to include a fourth person ("M"), only two months later, in March.

Since this is an experiment, and since we feel we have met with a good degree of success, I thought that a report summarizing the progress of our work would be of interest to other practitioners who similarly find themselves separated by miles but joined strongly by mutual interests. What follows then, are my comments upon our specific experiment and some of the practical lessons we've learned.

1: Methodology

Consensus process: We have no established hierarchy other than that which evolves naturally when unique individuals with a variety of talents, work together. Our decisions are made by a very unstructured process of group agreement. Bottom line is, we proceed only in directions that we have all agreed upon.

Shared commitment: We each share a basic commitment to pursuing this experiment through whatever twists and turns it may lead. An engaged and motivated interest in the project, seems essential to active participation.

Attitude of experimentation: We are engaged in this project to learn. We are not working to prove or disprove a particular personal agenda or dogma. Instead, we are working through trial and error, and with open minds, to learn what we can about astral meeting. Innovation, and the challenging and testing of our most basic assumptions, are the tools that we nurture. At the same time, wanting to ensure a high degree of consistency in our experiment, we have established the following controls.

Secrecy regarding astral locale: For very practical reasons, we have established a rule of confidentiality. We each agree not to share the details of our astral locale with anyone outside of our working circle. This is necessary because a description of our meeting site is the equivalent of an open invitation to join us! By maintaining this confidence, we retain control over who we share our astral locale with. Following consensus process, no one is invited to join us without the express agreement of all participants.

Communication by e-mail: Since we live so far away from each other, we rely almost exclusively upon e-mail communication. This means that only people with e-mail capability are currently participating. We find that e-mail: #1) simplifies the logistics of seeing that everyone gets a copy of every communication; #2) facilitates the archiving of our correspondence; and #3) makes last-minute scheduling an acceptable option.

Meeting schedule: We meet regularly at 10pm (Pacific Time) on the most mutually convenient night, as close to the actual New and Full Moons as we can manage. Our meetings last anywhere from 30 minutes to well over an hour. This establishes a predictable, yet not overwhelming, schedule of a minimum two meetings per calendar month. Often we meet for the Solstices and Equinoxes, or for personal reasons, so there are also months when we meet more than just twice. There was even a month when we managed to meet only once! Our basic commitment though, is to do our best to meet at each Full and New Moon. There is a special magic in attuning this way to so natural a rhythm as the Lunar cycle, and I highly recommend it! Not only has it established an easy rhythm for our meetings, it has also provided them a more powerful ritual context.

Independent reports: After a meeting, we each write a report describing our experience. There are only two rules regarding our reports: Rule #1) To maintain the control of independent reporting, we avoid reading the reports from other participants until we have completed writing our own. Rule #2) We do our best to submit our reports within three days of meeting. There are no rules pertaining to the format of our individual reports, and in fact, they vary widely in length and style. We encourage each other to be confident in our own peculiarities of self-expression!

Comparative discussion of reports: When all the reports from a given meeting have been submitted, we often (though not always) indulge in a critical comparison of them. We look for areas of commonality between our individual experiences, and assess the progress of our experiment. This process of critical analysis has frequently led to very important changes in our working methods. It is responsible for leading us to each of the most important lessons we've mastered regarding the evolution of our experiment. Experience has taught us that at each turn, we should examine what is and is not working, and then creatively modify our methods in accordance. Firmly rooted in the belief that each individual's experience is an equally valid component of the overall group-experience, we are never demeaning in our analysis of each other's reports. We nurture a working atmosphere of creativity by treating each other with a generous respect.

Archiving of reports and discussions: We save every bit of correspondence relative to our project for a number of reasons. First of all, it constitutes a detailed record of our experiment. Secondly, it provides us with a valuable perspective. Thirdly, our compendium of notes is required reading for new participants, and serves as both invitation and road map. We now publish a journal of each year's notes and issue updated supplements as needed (i.e., when new participants have joined us). These are distributed only to active participants. Our fourth reason for archiving our correspondence, is that we've learned it's a very satisfying thing to do. It provides us with a very tangible, evolving symbol of our otherwise intangible efforts, and this has had surprisingly positive effects upon our motivation when we've faced difficulty.

2: Establishing The Astral Locale

Assessment of needs: Before we chose our specific astral locale, we discussed our individual and joint needs. Assuming we were to actually succeed in meeting astrally, what sort of work would our locale need to accommodate? Would we eventually involve other people or would we need space only for two? These and other questions led us very quickly to choose a locale that was adaptable.

Natural setting vs. human-made structure: As I mentioned earlier, our choice was a natural, outdoor setting. We made this selection instinctively and without really understanding its consequences. Our desire was for a space with an "unlimited potential", but in finding such a setting, we encountered a different sort of limit -- our inability to encompass the illimitable!

The infinitude of details inherent in a natural setting overwhelmed our ability to arrive at a concise description of our locale. This is an important point, especially in the beginning, because (as experience has proven to us) the more concisely the details of the meeting place are known, the easier it is to reach a truly mutual experience.

A simple structure is easy to describe since there are a limited number of details to consider. But try to describe a natural, outdoor setting and you will find yourself making very general statements that offer more possibilities to the imagination than actual definitions. Our natural response to this situation has been to focus most of our work around specific sites within our larger locale. For instance, we spend much of our meeting time within the confines of a ritual circle that we have established. Our Circle has evolved to a consistent size, composed of a limited number of details, and is a place where we find it easy to attain a mutual focus.

Personally, I have established the habit of transiting first to an easily defined location within the confines of our overall astral locale. For this purpose, I employ an enclosure with a limited number of details with which I am intimately familiar. Once I have firmly established my presence there, I then venture outside and into the infinitude of Nature. Adopting this incremental progression from a stable, solitary environment into one which involves the greater vagaries of relationship, has been the key to my learning how to consistently maintain a grounded presence throughout an astral meeting.

My advice to one initiating an experiment such as this, is that you begin with a simple, though significantly meaningful, focal point for your meetings. An example would be our ritual Circle, or perhaps a simply built, though elegant, temple of some sort. Whatever suits your fancy, let its emphasis be upon simplicity at first. When you have succeeded at meeting in this easily defined locale, then venture outdoors, using your experiences inside your temple as the touchstone "reality" which you will then seek to duplicate amidst more natural surroundings.

Though it may require a bit more effort to manifest, a natural setting offers invaluable lessons, unattainable from within human-made confines. Quite simply, the inclusion of Nature opens the astral locale to The Mystery. I suggest that you experiment with a locale that ultimately offers both options.

Discovering vs. creating: Our choice of a natural setting immediately raised the question of whether we were going to create this locale or discover it. Two things factored into our decision. The first, was that we didn't want a human-made nature-substitute! We wanted Nature's own unique imprint, not just our best approximation. The second consideration was the very sure impression we both shared, that our locale existed prior to our arrival. Our very first experiences instilled a deep respect for our chosen locale -- for its sense of unique self-awareness. So we chose to explore our locale before undertaking any alterations to it, as a sign of our heart-felt respect. I have come to doubt that any other approach would work in the face of Nature!

We continue to explore even now, and are always making new discoveries.

As witnessed by our Circle, we have also indulged in slightly modifying our natural environment, to suit our particular needs. I say slightly, because our Circle existed as an outline in the grass, prior to our arrival, and all we have done is fill it in with details that help us focus. Had we chosen to begin with a limited structure (as I have advised you to do), we would have had to start with creating our Temple or Circle; and then shifted to exploration, only when we had emerged into the outdoors. However it is approached, the tool appropriate to Nature is exploration; and the tool appropriate to a focusing structure, is creation.

Imaging -- establishing the mental foundation: Hindsight is a wonderful luxury. With it, I can distill from our many trials and errors, a set of instructions based upon what eventually worked for us. For brevity's sake, I will focus upon what did work, and leave the amusingly fruitless parts to your imagination!

Step One: Clarify a mental image of your initial locale. If you are following my recommendation of starting with a defined structure, then define that structure in as minute detail as you can. Consider the measurement of its dimensions, the color and texture of its surfaces, the significance of each of its aspects, etc. Be as specific as your chosen locale will allow.

Experiencing -- establishing the astral reality: Step Two: Once you have the mental image defined, step into your locale and begin experiencing its details. This is accomplished by simply giving your astra-mental awareness a body that can function within your astral locale. Then focus your attention upon sensing all the details of your astral locale first-hand.

This will give astral substance to your mental image and build an intimate relationship between yourself and your locale. These first experiences with your locale should be solitary sessions, focused solely upon your individual impressions.

Describing and naming: Step Three: As you develop your personal relationship with the locale, communicate your impressions to the other participants who are also engaging in solitary exploration. Gradually integrate each participant's description, until you each arrive at an experience of the same details in your solitary ventures.

Step Four: When your solitary experiences match, try meeting together as a group.

Step Five: When your group meetings reflect a commonality of events as well as of environmental details, you should finalize the group-description of your locale and give it a name. Stabilize your environment in this way, and you will find it easier to consistently attain a high degree of commonality in your group experiences. As you make changes in your environment or discover new facets of it, be certain that all participants share an awareness of them.

3: Reaching The Established Astral Locale

Drawing a map with words: Your description of your astral locale is a map which can guide anyone to your meeting place, so preserve its confidentiality well. Treat it like you would a secret password, and reveal it only to those whom you intend to invite into your group's work.

To reach your locale, begin by bringing its description and name into your mind, and concentrate on building a mental connection.

Creative visualization: Boiled down to its simplest terms, you reach your astral locale by consciously placing yourself within its set of details. This is done through the creative visualization of your locale's environment and the shifting of your awareness firmly into it. Experience has shown that there are any number of ways to accomplish this. Each one of the participants in our experiment, has practiced a slightly different technique, but common to them all is that we start with the mental connection and build from there.

Mental and astral travel: In analyzing the various techniques we've employed, I see them as falling into two distinct categories. The simplest approach is that of mental travel, in which one sits quietly and projects only one's mind to the astral locale. The more complex approach involves consciously projecting one's astral form to the locale. Astral travel produces a much richer experience and opens one to levels of sensory perception impossible without the astral body; but it is by far, a more difficult density of presence to attain with consistency. Therefore I recommend that you begin with the easier mental projection, and work gradually toward the goal of an astral presence.

Dealing with distractions: As you shift your awareness away from your physical body and towards your astral locale, you will invariably encounter distractions. The most primary distraction is a wandering mind. For example, you sit to focus on your locale's details and find yourself considering your grocery list instead. When this occurs, it is important to avoid indulging in a frustration-based reaction. Instead, approach this sort of distraction as an opportunity for the creative strengthening of your mental discipline.

The first step in overcoming a distraction of any sort, is to recognize that you are indeed distracted. Briefly define what distracts you, and then willfully turn your attention away from the distraction and back towards the details of your astral locale. Consciously exercising your power to choose your mind's focus, directly strengthens your mental discipline. With practice, it becomes an easy matter to return your attention to its original focus and to then keep it there undisturbed by extraneous thoughts.

While your mind is focused elsewhere, you will still receive occasional sensory messages from your physical body. Loud noises; sudden changes in light intensity; strong aromas; bodily discomforts; the need to sneeze, belch, cough, fart, etc.; and most especially, being physically touched by another person or animal; are examples of physical distractions. Many of these items can be avoided by choosing your meditation space wisely, but even the most isolated quiet-room cannot free you from sensing this annoying itch or that cramped muscle!

When a physical distraction imposes itself upon your awareness, respond as with a mental distraction and begin by first recognizing the distraction. If what has distracted you is the sound of someone breaking and entering, then by all means terminate your meditation and address the distraction directly! If it is only something on the par of a passing car's headlights, then release your focus upon it and return to your meditation. Each such distraction will require a moment of decision in which you must gauge its importance and determine your response. It is often less distracting in the long run to scratch that itch, than to struggle with ignoring it. Whatever the specific circumstance, it is important to approach a distraction calmly and to immediately regain control over your choice of focus.

Each successful dealing with a distraction increases the strength of your internal discipline. To a certain extent, this results in fewer actual distractions, but it will never totally free one from having to deal with them. Experience has shown me that the key to maintaining a consistent density of presence throughout an astral meeting, is not found in the avoidance of distractions; but rather, is to be found in creatively addressing those distractions. Now, when I am presented with the need to cough for instance, I am able to process the distraction with a specific portion of my awareness and I am generally not required to shift my whole focus back to my physical body. If I then cough as my body is urging me to, it does not significantly interrupt my astral experience. Trial and error experimentation has taught me to process distractions very swiftly, and in such a manner that they no longer detract from my chosen focus.

The final category of distraction that I will note, concerns astral travel specifically. When one separates one's astral form from one's physical body, the physical body itself experiences an initial fear. Quite simply, it is the fear of death, as experienced at the cellular level of biologically inherited instinct. The astral separation so closely mimics the process of physical death, that the physical body responds with an initial panic. At first this is a barrier to successful astral travel, as it tends to draw one immediately back into the physical. Treated with the same directness and creativity that I have suggested regarding mental and physical distractions, this barrier is eventually overcome.

With repeated practice, your physical body will learn that its fear is generally unnecessary. I say generally, because in your astral travels, you may find that certain experiences re-ignite this physical fear response. The consciousness of the solitary physical body (i.e., from which you have separated your mental and astral bodies) is relatively primitive and animalistic. Very like a domesticated pet, the physical body's consciousness learns to trust and to release its instinctual fear only after experiences have affirmed for it the trustworthiness of its master. Such trust is always weighed against instinct and so it is never absolute.

Increasing your astral presence: Travelling with your astral body opens you to a range of sensory perception very similar to what you experience with your physical body. Mental travel on the other hand, allows only for sight and a form of mental hearing, and there is a marked absence of spontaneous tactile sensations. Therefore, to increase your astral presence at your locale, concentrate upon using your astral senses to perceive your astral surroundings. Feel the astral floor/ground beneath your astral feet; feel the movement of your astral limbs; sense the temperature and smell of the astral air; touch the different astral surfaces around you. In this way, you will clarify your surroundings and increase the intimacy of your contact with them.

An aspect of the astral sensoria which does not have a physical parallel, is what I call the "astral speak/feel". This organ of perception is tied primarily into the astral organs of sight and hearing. Speak/feel allows one to look at an astral object and receive from it an audio-visual communication that is filled with intimate details, feelings, thoughts, etc. I find that using this specifically astral sense, increases my astral presence dramatically. With practice, I have found it easy to tie all my astral senses into the speak/feel, increasing the range of information perceived to include touch and smell as well. At each level of the speak/feel, the information perceived is felt emotionally; and at the same time, processed intellectually.

Speak/feel is an organ of communication -- of perception and expression. One can, with practice, learn to project one's own unique speak/feel message, and converse in this way with the astral surroundings. One of my most blissful memories is of a speak/feel conversation with a meadow of grasses -- I perceived such indescribable joyousness! I recommend a speak/feel conversation with your astral locale as the most potent way to increase your astral presence.

4: Experiencing The Astral Locale

Projection vs. "reality": There is one unavoidable question inherent in this sort of experiment. In fact, it forms the very foundation of our approach. The question we each ask ourselves every time we venture to our astral locale is: Are my experiences and perceptions merely delusions, projected by my active imagination; or do they reflect actual events and things?

Moved by this question, several occult Traditions have devised techniques for testing or proving an astral or mental vision. Beyond the fact that they introduce an element of challenge and focus one's attention upon this central question, I don't think they are themselves proof from self-delusion. Repeated experiment and the experiences which result, are what truly teach one to discern a self-deluded projection from a genuine experience of your astral locale.

I know of no better, more powerful an aid to answering this question than receiving a second, or third, or fourth, opinion! When we share the reports of our group meetings, we get a chance to see if our experiences in any way matched those of the other participants. Instances of commonality have led us to perfect our methods, resulting in less self-delusion and greater mutuality evinced in our reports.

The high degree of commonality that we have achieved satisfies us presently. From these successes, we are learning to trust our process and our results -- but like the domesticated pet I mentioned earlier, our trust is by no means absolute and we question it at every turn.

In the beginning of our experiment, I focused closely on discerning my projections from the astral reality. I ended up spending a couple of meetings completely obsessed with the issue, and these were the most delusional of all! I learned quickly that my very correct attitude of questioning was unfortunately being applied at an incorrect stage. It seems that the proper stage for analysis is actually after an astral meeting. During the meeting itself, it was clear that I should trust and experience whatever came, and save the critical dissection for the discussion of our reports. For it was clearly from the post-report discussions that we were learning the lessons which were bringing us closer to a truly mutual experience. I determined to "act now, analyze later", and have been so impressed by the results of this approach that I hold to it even now.

One of the greatest barriers to achieving a non-projected experience is too tight a hold on your preconceptions. Your expectations as to what will or will not happen can easily lead you into a self-deluded projection. This is especially true when you experience things that don't fall within your frame of reference. A natural response is to begin translating them into symbols which fit your understanding. This tends to, at the very least, limit your experience -- and once you reach the limits of your understanding, removes you to your own expectation-based fantasy.

Levels of commonality: An area which has tested nearly every one of our preconceptions has been our search for commonality in our meetings. We learned that discerning commonality in an astral setting is a far different matter than when judging it in a physical setting. In a physical setting we make broad assumptions, based upon the evidence of our trusted physical senses, that when several individuals come together, they experience commonality in their perceptions. There is a subtle and generally unquestioned agreement that each person present sees the same surroundings. In our astral setting however, this basic degree of commonality is missing and we are relying on our less trusted astral and mental senses.

Upon closer examination, the commonality that we assume occurs in a shared physical setting, breaks down when each of the individuals present describes what they perceive. Vast differences will be seen between the descriptions of both the surroundings and the events. This reveals how utterly personal, perception really is. As each person views a particular feature or experiences a particular shared event, it will raise a unique set of thoughts and emotional responses. In effect, we each see a common universe, but in divergent ways. Our perceptions often diverge radically when it comes to our emotional impressions and our subsequent thought processes.

Experience has taught us to look for three levels of commonality in our meetings:

Level One: Meaning -- This is the most basic level of commonality and also the most difficult to analyze rationally. For example: in one meeting I ritually cast our circle, using standard techniques shared by Wiccan and Hermetic traditions. This was perceived differently by each of the other participants .

T, who had the least familiarity with myself and with the techniques I was employing, perceived it as candles being lit at each quarter of our circle and as a general feeling of "things coming together." Even though there was no agreement on the flow of events, nor upon any of the minute details, the meaning of her experience certainly matched my real-time actions.

Over and over, we have learned the lesson that we each perceive astral events through the lens of our own unique internal symbol-language. Analyzing our reports has meant that we've had to learn each other's language and idiom, and then translate, often intuitively, into the language of essential-meaning shared by all. At this level, we have achieved at least 90% commonality in our meetings over a two year span.

Level Two: Flow of events -- Here, not only is there a sharing of essential-meaning, but also the rhythm and sequence of events is shared. For example, the same ritualized circle casting was perceived by M (with whom I am closely acquainted) as a series of specific actions that enlivened and ignited our circle. Even though she had very little familiarity with the specific techniques I employed, she clearly described the sequence of my ritual casting and its essential meaning. She did not however, perceive the details of what I was doing. At this level, we have achieved a 60% commonality in our meetings over a two year span.

Level Three: Minute detail -- This is the most comprehensive and easily analyzed level of commonality. It is also the least common in our meetings, occurring perhaps only 30% of the time. For example, my ritual circle casting was perceived by K in minute detail, 90% of which matched my real-time actions. Unlike my relationship with T and M though, K and I speak a more similar internal symbol-language, having both studied and practiced some similar magical traditions. In short, the greater the similarity between the symbol-languages of the participants, the greater the degree of commonality in perception of events.

Synchronizing time and place: When we want to meet with someone physically, we simply state a place and time for our rendezvous, and at the correct time we arrive at the chosen location. It's a very straight forward proposition in the physical world, but in the astral realm, time and place are vagaries determined by intention and attention, rather than the certainties of physical laws.

Syncing place in the astral realm is simply a matter of intentionally visualizing the same astral locale. However, it does little toward reaching a commonality of experience to meet at the same place but at different times! Carefully syncing the astral time of your meeting will greatly increase your chances for commonality.

In a natural setting, this is fairly easily achieved through all participants visualizing the same season, time of day and phase of the moon. In a man-made, indoor setting, you must build in some feature which will help you determine the time -- perhaps a clock of some sort or a window through which you can view the sky.

Working together at the same moment in physical time aids in the syncing of the astral time, and is by far the best course to pursue. However, it is not essential. Experience has proven that it is possible to project back in physical-time terms, to the ever-present astral moment of meeting, and then engage in a real-time experience of events.

K was the first of our group to explore this possibility. One month, he had missed our Full Moon meeting and decided to attend on the following evening. He projected his awareness to our astral locale with the intention of arriving at the moment, 24 hours earlier, when our Full Moon meeting began. To everyone's surprise, his report of that meeting displayed no less commonality than usual! We had all perceived his presence, even though it was a projection from a time yet to occur in our experience. He likewise had accurately perceived our meeting and had even engaged in shaping the real-time flow of events within a time that had already occurred.

This practice works best when going back in time to a meeting that has passed, but is less advantageous when a meeting has yet to occur and one is attempting to reach forward in time. While either journey through time is possible in the astral and (even more so) in the mental realms, the possibility of self-delusion seems to increase the further into the future one strays.

My advice is that you first develop the discipline of working together in real-time before experimenting with astra-mental time travel.

A final aspect of syncing in astral time is noting the passage of time during the meeting. Astra-mental time does not flow with the inexorable regularity of physical time. The measure of astra-mental time is dependent upon the intensity of the ideas and emotions the experience encompasses. It is therefore uneven, irregular and unpredictable, unlike physical time. At first this fact can be disorienting as you find only half an hour of physical time has passed during an astra-mental experience encompassing many "hours" of events. By noting the physical time you began your meeting and the physical time you returned to full bodily consciousness, and then comparing it's length to the perceived passage of astra-mental time, you will eventually come to understand the connection between these two different aspects of time. This discipline will greatly increase your ability to sync with others in astra-mental time.

Working together: Learning how to come together astra-mentally, though a great and rewarding labor in its own right, is only the first step. The second, even more challenging step is to learn to work together effectively within your astra-mental environment. Once we had mastered the first step to our satisfaction, the question arose: "What now?" The answer was obvious: "Do something."

The first action we undertook that went beyond simply arriving together at the same astra-mental time-place, was to pursue a joint focus upon a simple object. For us, this object was a specific bird's feather, one that we were all familiar with and could therefore visualize with equal clarity of detail. Any simple object will do as long as all the participants agree upon the details ahead of time.

We have come to call this our "feather focus" and we usually begin our meetings with a few minutes sitting around our feather, focusing upon it in unison. This has the effect of bringing us together into very close mutual proximity to the exact same moment of astra-mental space. Not only are we intentionally syncing at the levels of meaning and flow of events, but also very clearly at the level of minute detail.

Even though the differences between our initial striving to reach the same astral-mental moment, and our subsequent feather-focus, are subtle, they are nonetheless significant. They represent a more proactive group-approach to the astral locale.

A very natural result of any group of people binding its attention upon a common focus, is the multiplication of energy. This is very noticeable at the astra-mental level and can produce significant physical effects if the level of energy generated exceeds the personal limits of the participants. We've each succeeded in making ourselves physically nauseous, dizzy, or overloaded with vibrant energy, at one point or another during this project! Each time we experienced this sort of physical discomfort, it was due to our exceeding our own limits of tolerance. From this we have learned to protect ourselves and to carefully stretch our limits in small increments.

I recommend that you approach this natural multiplication of energy very consciously and with a moderate degree of caution. Begin

150

by joining hands in a circle at your astral locale and cast your attention to a mutually agreed upon object. When you are all well focused together, take careful note of the group's energy level as well as your own personal level.

Now gently and mutually begin to circulate a current of energy clockwise (deosil) around your hand-held circle. Maintain a personally comfortable level of energy flow for a few minutes, one that does not stretch your limits.

Another way of putting it, is that you should allow only a comfortable amount of the group's energy to reach you. If there is more energy available than you can comfortably handle, then consciously limit what you accept into your own astra-mental body. This is simply a matter of conscious intention; of willing it to be so and making it so.

When you have acclimated yourself to this comfortable level, then open yourself to a little more of the group's energy and slowly stretch your limits of comfort. As your limits stretch, so will your ability to consciously work with this energy toward creative ends.

Once you agree, as a group, that you have reached a state where you can work directly with the group energy you raise, plan a specific task for that energy. An example might be a simple sharing of healing energy, or perhaps a more complex ritual of some sort. I suggest you start simply and work your way up to the more complex options as the need arises.

Create uses for your group's energy that satisfy real and present needs. This guarantees that you will be able to gauge your effectiveness by verifying whether or not there were any tangible results. For example, choosing a vague project such as world peace, while certainly noble, guarantees that you will have little upon which to gauge the effectiveness of your group working. Practicality and innovation will more thoroughly engage your group's interest.

Possibilities: There are immense possibilities inherent in an astral locale simply due to the fact that it is built of the astra-mental substance. This substance has infinite potential and offers us the opportunity to explore whatever possibility we can imagine.

At its most basic level, an astral locale offers an immense opportunity for learning about the universe and the self. It is a realm which, if nothing else, supports the enacting of cathartic psycho-dramas which can reconnect one to an inner source of deep personal wisdom.

It is an ideal setting in which to carry out ritual workings and even long-range magical projects. For example, it could serve as a valuable supplement to a correspondence course in magical training in which actual lodge-work was impossible.

The possibilities are truly limited only by the imagination! The tool of imagination and its natural process of limiting the astra-mental substance, is what allows us the ability to realize the astra-mental substance's potentials. Creative innovation is by far the most productive tact when pursuing this sort of work.

5: Introducing New Participants

When K and I had reached a satisfactory success in our astral meeting project, we decided to open our experiment and include at least one other person in our workings. We felt it was time to see what effect a third person would have upon our overall experiment and upon the astral locale itself.

The whole process was very gratifying and greatly enriched our astral-meeting experience. Even though the first person we invited left the group (amicably) only six months later, we felt that the benefits that came from enlarging our group were worth the effort involved. Since that time, we have successfully integrated two other participants into our group, bringing our current number of active participants to four.

Our three efforts at opening our group have taught us some valuable lessons. We found that there are four basic factors to consider: 1) Finding one's place in an already established group dynamic is a difficult and often intimidating task. Great care needs to be taken in warmly welcoming a new participant. 2) Likewise, it is often difficult for an established group dynamic to open itself to the change which a new face brings. The group must remain acutely aware of its tendency toward inertia and actively embrace the opposite pole of openness-to-change. 3) There are logistic considerations such as making sure the printed materials reach the new participant and that they are informed of meeting times, techniques, etc. 4) Each new participant will naturally cause the astral locale to change slightly. Just as the original group shapes the locale, so also will the addition of a new perspective to some extent re-shape that locale. A balance must be struck between respecting the established locale and openness to growth.

Our experiences quickly led us to establish a well defined process for introducing new participants. It has worked successfully both of the times we've followed it, so I recommend it to you.

The role of guide: Central to our process of integrating a new participant into our group is the concept of sponsorship. Each candidate has one person from the established group who will act as initial liaison and guide. This guide is the candidate's entry into the group dynamic; and likewise, the guide is the group's entry into the inevitable change of it's own dynamic.

The guide is responsible for getting the introductory material (a copy of our Journal) to the candidate and in every other way facilitating their inclusion into the group meetings. However, this role should terminate once the candidate has successfully met with the group at the astral locale. It is not meant to be a long-term hierarchical role; instead, it's to be one of advocacy and warm welcoming. Once welcomed though, the candidate becomes an equal participant.

In our experience, the role of guide was necessary for only the first two months after the initial invitation to join. Despite its brevity, it is still a crucial role. I advise against opening your group to new participants if there are no members of your group willing to commit the time and effort required for this role. In that case, it is best to wait till someone is available for the task.

Selection and invitation: When a member of our group proposes someone as a candidate, we must all agree upon their inclusion before we offer that person an invitation. I must confess that in practice, the person who proposes the candidate ends up acting as the primary guide for that candidate.

I have proposed two candidates -- one who stayed with us for six months and one who has been with us for almost a year now -- and I'm considering two others. What they all share is a strong interest in the idea of our astral meeting project and that is my primary criteria for candidacy. For example, M repeatedly stated her interest and inquired for over a year as to the project's progress. The other two I'm considering for inclusion in our group have expressed a similar consistency and depth of interest in the project.

Other important questions are: Am I personally interested in working on such an intimate level with this person? Would they really benefit from participation? Does this person realistically have the free-time available in their busy lives to commit to the project?

Once group consensus has been reached on a candidate, the guide proffers an invitation. If accepted, the candidate is sent a copy of our Journal-to-date. This is a detailed record of our work and open' with a description of our astral locale.

Solitary exploration: As the candidate reads our Journal's descriptions, they will naturally begin to formulate a mental picture of, and an emotional relationship with, our astral locale. This marks the beginning of a phase of solitary exploration wherein the candidate attempts to more and more clearly reach the astral locale on their own. The candidate works at building a personal connection with the locale.

First two-person meeting: Should the candidate have difficulty reaching the astral locale, or conversely, when the candidate has successfully reached the locale, a meeting at the astral locale between the candidate and the guide should be arranged. At least one two-person meeting should be attempted before attempting a full-group meeting. If there are problems, then a series of two-person meetings should be pursued until the difficulties are resolved.

First group meeting: Once the two-person meeting goes well, it is time for the candidate to attempt joining in the regular full-group meeting. The established group should take care that the candidate does not exceed their limits and become overwhelmed by the group's energy. Likewise the candidate should remain conscientious of their own limits and not exceed them.

When and if the candidate succeeds in joining the group meeting, they cease to be a candidate (assuming no one raises an objection) and they become an equal participant.

Epilogue

I hope my words encourage you to engage in a similar work. The rewards far, far outweigh the effort required! And the work, though it may sound overwhelming and complex, is really quite an easy labor.

December 21st, 1997 marked two years of meeting at our astral locale. Our project continues to evolve and we are presently moving toward a more relaxed approach to our meetings. In many ways, we are letting go of the "project" part of our work and simply focusing on the "work" part.

Index

Color Plates

Malkuth: Entrance

Malkuth: Tunnel

Malkuth: Temple

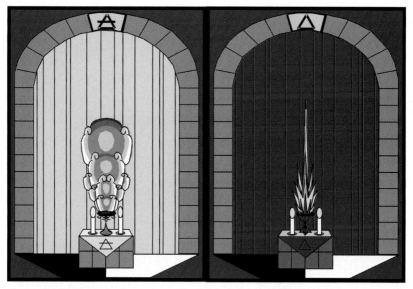

Malkuth: Air Altar   **Malkuth: Fire Altar**

Malkuth: Earth Altar   **Malkuth: Water Altar**

Yesod: Altar

Yesod: Temple

Hod: Altar

Hod: Temple

Netzach: Altar

Netzach: Temple

Tiphareth: Altar

Tiphareth: Temple

Geburah: Altar

Geburah: Temple

Gedulah: Altar

Gedulah: Temple

Binah: Altar